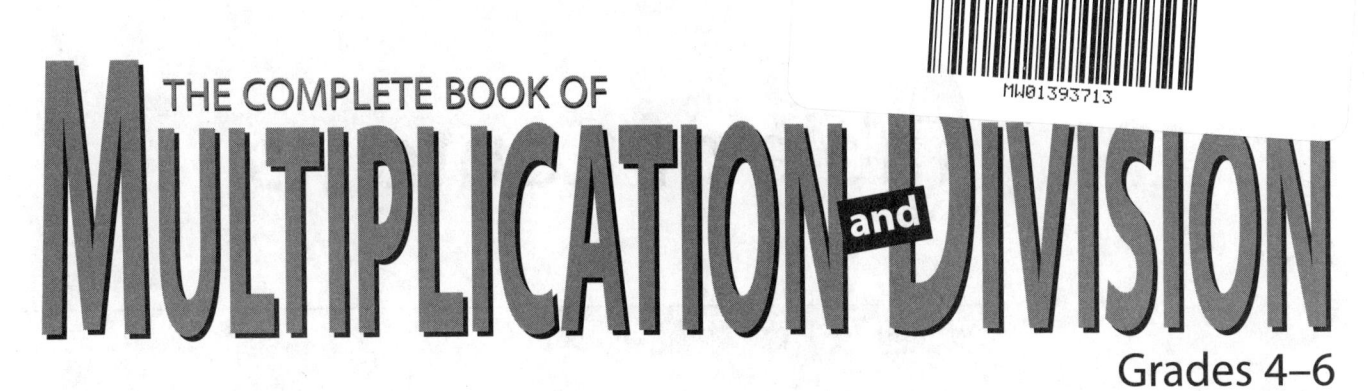

THE COMPLETE BOOK OF MULTIPLICATION and DIVISION

Grades 4–6

Written by
Hy Kim, Ed.D.

Editors: Teri L. Applebaum and Sheri Rous
Illustrator: Corbin Hillam
Cover Illustrator: Moonhee Pak
Designer/Production: Moonhee Pak/Rosa Gandara
Cover Designer: Moonhee Pak
Art Director: Tom Cochrane
Project Director: Carolea Williams

© 2004 Creative Teaching Press, Inc., Huntington Beach, CA 92649
Reproduction of activities in any manner for use in the classroom and not for commercial sale is permissible.
Reproduction of these materials for an entire school or for a school system is strictly prohibited.

Table of Contents

Introduction 3

GETTING STARTED

How to Use This Book 4
Differentiated Instruction 6
NCTM Standards Correlation 7

LESSON PLANS AND ACTIVITIES

Teach Basic Facts
Lesson 1: Multiply with 0, 1, and 10 8
Lesson 2: Multiply with 2 11
Lesson 3: Multiply with 5 14
Lesson 4: Multiply with 9 17
Lesson 5: Multiply with 4 20
Lesson 6: Multiply with 3 23
Lesson 7: Multiply with 6 26
Lesson 8: Multiply with 7 and 8 29
Lesson 9: Divide by 2 and 3 32
Lesson 10: Divide by 4, 5, and 6 35
Lesson 11: Divide by 7, 8, and 9 38

Teach More Advanced Concepts
Lesson 12: Mental Math and Multiples 41
Lesson 13: Prime and Composite Numbers 47
Lesson 14: Multiply by Multiples of 10 53
Lesson 15: Multiply by Two-Digit Numbers 59
Lesson 16: Estimate Products Using Compatible Factors 65
Lesson 17: Divide Multiples of 10 71
Lesson 18: Divide by Tens 77
Lesson 19: Divide with Two-Digit Divisors 83
Lesson 20: Square Numbers and Square Roots 89
Lesson 21: Least Common Multiple and Least Common Denominator 95
Lesson 22: Multiply with Decimals 101
Lesson 23: Sales Tax and Sale Price 107
Lesson 24: Estimate Percents Using Compatible Numbers 113
Lesson 25: Prime Factorization 119
Lesson 26: Divide with Decimals 125

ASSESSMENT

Teacher Record Sheet 131
Pretest 132
Cumulative Test 134

Answer Key 135

Introduction

The Complete Book of Multiplication and Division provides all the necessary tools to review basic multiplication and division and introduce students to more advanced number theories that build on their basic fact knowledge. This resource guide features 11 lessons that contain strategies to help students review and master basic multiplication and division facts and 15 lessons to teach them to apply this knowledge to more advanced concepts. Learning math is a developmental process. That is why each lesson in this book focuses on a specific skill to enable students to build on prior knowledge as they learn a new concept. Each lesson is tied to the National Council of Teachers of Mathematics (NCTM) standards. Before you begin to teach a lesson, refer to the NCTM Standards Correlation chart on page 7 to identify the standards you will be teaching.

Each lesson includes a complete, simple-to-use lesson plan. The teacher pages in lessons 1–11 include objectives for student learning, direct instruction, guided practice, and assessment to provide students with a review of basic facts and practice for students who have not yet achieved mastery. The teacher pages in lessons 12–26 consist of objectives for student learning, direct instruction, guided practice, independent practice, and assessment as students are introduced to more advanced multiplication and division concepts. These components will provide thorough instruction to students as they are introduced to the new skills through a whole-class lesson, as they practice the new skills with your assistance and then independently, and as they complete a quiz to assess their comprehension. Use the Answer Key (pages 135–144) to check students' work on all the quizzes, tests, and practice pages in this resource.

Throughout this book, students are taught to use a thinking or reasoning approach rather than solely rote memory. To help them with this approach, lessons emphasize the use of manipulatives and pictures as well as the use of making connections to prior knowledge. Students are also encouraged to use mental math to help them achieve mastery of new concepts. This book is filled with interactive practice activities and games for partners, small groups, and the whole class to keep students actively participating in the learning process and to keep them motivated and excited about learning multiplication and division.

You will be amazed at how easily students will learn to use multiplication and division as you incorporate the lessons in this book into your everyday math curriculum. Your students will feel a sense of excitement and accomplishment each time they master a new skill area and will be overjoyed when they are congratulated on their achievement!

How to Use This Book

Before you begin teaching the lessons in this resource book, take time to review the Table of Contents and the NCTM Standards Correlation chart (page 7) to help you understand what skills and standards will be met as you teach each lesson. Read through the following information to get a better feeling for the format of each lesson and the activities that are included in each and their purpose. Also, read the information on differentiated instruction (page 6) so you can plan ahead of time how to meet the needs of *all* the students in your classroom.

LESSONS

The first 11 lessons in this book review basic multiplication and division facts with students. The next 15 lessons introduce students to more advanced concepts that build upon their basic fact knowledge. For that reason, begin with lesson 1 if students need basic fact review. If students have mastered their basic facts, begin with lesson 12.

- **Lessons 1–8** teach basic multiplication facts and **lessons 9–11** teach basic division facts and help students make the connection between multiplication and division by introducing them to fact families. Each lesson includes teacher directions, a student practice page, and a quiz to assess their mastery.
- **Lessons 12–26** introduce students to more advanced number theory concepts. It is important that students have mastery of their basic facts prior to their introduction to these new concepts because these lessons teach students to apply their basic facts knowledge to more advanced concepts (i.e., dividing with two-digit divisors). Each of these lessons includes teacher directions, student practice pages, games, and a quiz to assess their mastery.

As students are introduced to new concepts, review prior lessons or basic knowledge that will help them master the new concept. Continually assess students' understanding and make adjustments to your teaching based on students' needs (see Differentiated Instruction on page 6).

EXTENSIONS

✓ If students need additional practice with basic facts, create sets of flash cards for partners or for students to take home to practice with their family. You can also use flash cards in a game format for use with the whole class. Choose five students to sit in chairs at the front of the classroom. Choose five more students to stand behind the seated students. Invite the remaining students to form a line. Challenge each pair (sitting vs. standing) to be the first to correctly answer the fact on a flash card. Have the winner of each pair sit down in the chair, and invite the students in the line to replace the standing students. (Have all of the standing students remain where they are until after the fifth pair has answered their question. Then, ask all of the students who are non-winners to walk to the back of the line together to avoid bad feelings.)

✓ Invite students to create their own word problems, similar to the ones students complete on the Problem Solving & Practice pages throughout lessons 12–26. Have students switch word problems with a partner and try to correctly answer their partner's problems. This type of activity will further increase students' mastery of new concepts because students will practice the new concept and internalize its rules and steps as they create their own word problems as well as when they solve someone else's problems.

How to Use This Book

ASSESSMENT

✓ Pretest, quizzes, and a cumulative test are all included in this book.

✓ **Pretest (pages 132–133):** Use this after reviewing basic multiplication and division facts with students (lessons 1–11) or prior to teaching each advanced concept lesson (lessons 12–26). There are two questions to assess students' knowledge of each skill in lessons 12–26.

✓ **Quizzes:** Each lesson ends with a quiz with questions to assess students' mastery of the newly learned skill. Many quizzes also contain ten review questions to assess their retention of past skills. Challenge students to complete each test several times, quicker each time. Or, give each student a quiz and announce the time at 30-second or 1-minute intervals. Students who finish within that interval can write the time at the top of their paper and turn it over.

✓ **Cumulative Test (page 134):** The questions assess students' ability to answer questions based on each lesson in this book.

✓ **Teacher Record Sheet (page 131):** Keep records for the whole class or individual students.

✓ **Whole Class:** Write each student's name on the left side of the chart. Each time students take a test or quiz, record their results in the corresponding column.

✓ **Individuals:** Copy a chart for each student. Have students take the quizzes several times (as suggested in the lessons) to challenge them to "beat their time" and show their mastery of the skill. Write the date the student took the quiz on the left side of the chart, and record his or her score in the corresponding column. This individualized chart will provide a "running record" of students' growth throughout the school year.

Differentiated Instruction

Each lesson in this book begins with objectives for student learning. Because students learn differently, and at different rates, it is important to differentiate your instruction to meet the needs of *all* your students. The activities in each lesson enable you to do this.

Each lesson begins with a teacher lesson plan and includes student practice pages, games, problem-solving activities (lessons 12–26), and a quiz. It is important to realize that differentiated instruction does NOT mean you need to teach each student separately. It is more accurate to refer to it as a method of presenting the same skill or topic to all your students through several different learning experiences to enhance each student's ability to "get it."

Lessons 12–26 provide you with a whole-class lesson, guided practice, independent practice, and assessment. Some students may need more guided practice while some may need more independent practice. Shape the method of presentation and practice of activities within the lessons to fit the needs of your students. Have some students independently complete reproducibles that are presented as guided practice and others complete with teacher assistance reproducibles that are presented as independent practice. It is important for you to use the strategies and methods presented for learning concepts in a way that helps your students achieve and be successful!

A suggested time limit is given for each quiz at the end of a lesson. Use this time limit as a guideline for your assessment. Provide additional time for students who need it, and challenge other students to "beat their time" and complete the quiz with 90–100% accuracy in a shorter amount of time.

Give students a sense of ownership in their learning and assessment. Copy all of the pages in a lesson and staple them together to make a packet for each student. Invite students to complete the pages one at a time, beginning with the first page. Once they have completed a reproducible, have them check their answers on pages 135–144. Ask students to circle the answers they got wrong and to show you their paper. Discuss the incorrect problems with them and any questions they may have. Then, have students redo the incorrect problems until they correctly answer them. Tell students to record on the Teacher Record Sheet (page 131) how many they missed on their first try. When students are ready to complete an activity for partners, tell them to write their name on the chalkboard and work with another student who is at the same stage. This process will allow students to work at their own pace and receive help when they need it. It will also provide you with time to meet individually with students to assess their understanding as well as provide you with a visual record of your students' achievement through a skill area.

Differentiated instruction allows you to plan your teaching to meet the needs of all your students by assessing where they are and moving forward in a direction that will help them achieve. By presenting the lessons and activities this way, you will make learning accessible to every student in your classroom and allow each one to shine as he or she masters a new skill!

NCTM Standards Correlation

	Lesson 1	Lesson 2	Lesson 3	Lesson 4	Lesson 5	Lesson 6	Lesson 7	Lesson 8	Lesson 9	Lesson 10	Lesson 11	Lesson 12	Lesson 13	Lesson 14	Lesson 15	Lesson 16	Lesson 17	Lesson 18	Lesson 19	Lesson 20	Lesson 21	Lesson 22	Lesson 23	Lesson 24	Lesson 25	Lesson 26
Arrays		•			•			•												•						
Basic Division Facts									•	•	•							•	•	•	•					
Basic Multiplication Facts	•	•	•	•	•	•	•	•	•	•	•	•	•	•	•	•	•				•	•	•	•	•	•
Decimals																•							•	•	•	•
Divide with Two-Digit Divisors																		•	•							•
Division									•	•	•							•	•	•	•					•
Estimation																•			•					•		
Fact Families									•	•	•															
Factoring													•			•									•	
Fractions																					•		•			
Least Common Denominator																					•					
Least Common Multiple																					•					
Mental Math													•					•								
Money			•			•			•									•				•				•
Multiples													•		•	•		•	•		•					
Multiplication		•	•	•	•	•	•	•	•				•	•	•	•	•				•	•	•	•	•	•
Multiply by Two or More Digits													•		•	•	•					•	•	•		
Percents																							•	•		
Prime Numbers														•											•	
Square Numbers & Roots																				•						

LESSON 1

Multiply with 0, 1, and 10

OBJECTIVES

Students will be introduced to the concept of multiplication as repeated addition. Students will master multiplication of 0, 1, and 10.

DIRECT INSTRUCTION

Teach students to create mental images of multiplication problems as repeated addition problems. Write on the board *0 + 0 = ?* Ask students how many zeroes they see. Write *2 x __ = ?* Ask what number is repeated two times. Write *0* on the line and as the answer. Tell students to read the multiplication problem as 2 zeroes are 0 and to picture two zeroes in their head. This will help them see multiplication number sentences as repeated addition. Write *0 + 0 + 0 = ?* Discuss its conversion to *3 x 0 = ?* and its mental image of three zeroes. Repeat this for 4 x 0 up to 10 x 0. After discussing the zero times tables, repeat the process with 1 + 1 = 2 and its conversion to 2 x 1 = 2 (2 ones are 2) up to 10 x 1 = 10 (10 ones are 10) to introduce the one times tables. Introduce the ten times tables in the same way. For each problem, ask students how the multiplication problem should be read (e.g., 5 zeroes are 0, 2 tens are 20) and what they should picture in their head (e.g., five zeroes, two tens).

Discuss what the numbers in any multiplication problem mean. Write on the board *2 x 10 = 20*. Tell students that the 2 means how many tens there are (the number of groups or sets) and the 10 means how many numbers (objects) are in each group. Write on the board several addition problems and multiplication problems (using zero, one, or ten). Ask students to convert repeated addition into multiplication and vice versa. For example, write *4 x 1 = 4* and have students convert it to *1 + 1 + 1 + 1 = 4*. Have them explain the meaning of each problem. (Use manipulatives or draw pictures to help students who are having difficulty.)

GUIDED PRACTICE

✓ Work with students in small groups to help them complete the **0, 1, and 10 Skill Practice reproducible (page 9)**. Challenge students to write their own rules at the bottom of the page.

ASSESSMENT

✓ Have students complete the **Lesson 1 Quiz (page 10)** in 2 minutes. Challenge students to "beat their time" and complete the quiz in 1 minute and then again in 30 seconds to show that they have mastered the number facts.

Name_____ Date_____

0, 1, and 10 Skill Practice

Match related number sentences. Write the correct letter on each line.

7 × 0 _____
9 × 1 _____
4 × 10 _____
10 × 0 _____
3 × 0 _____
6 × 1 _____
6 × 10 _____

a) 1 + 1 + 1 + 1 + 1 + 1 + 1 + 1 + 1
b) 10 + 10 + 10 + 10 + 10 + 10
c) 0 + 0 + 0
d) 10 + 10 + 10 + 10
e) 1 + 1 + 1 + 1 + 1 + 1
f) 0 + 0 + 0 + 0 + 0 + 0 + 0
g) 0 + 0 + 0 + 0 + 0 + 0 + 0 + 0 + 0 + 0

Write the answers.

h	1 × 0 =	1 × 1 =	1 × 10 =	4 × 1 =
i	2 × 0 =	2 × 1 =	2 × 10 =	2 × 0 =
j	3 × 0 =	3 × 1 =	3 × 10 =	1 × 10 =
k	4 × 0 =	4 × 1 =	4 × 10 =	5 × 1 =
l	5 × 0 =	5 × 1 =	5 × 10 =	9 × 10 =
m	6 × 0 =	6 × 1 =	6 × 10 =	6 × 1 =
n	7 × 0 =	7 × 1 =	7 × 10 =	7 × 0 =
o	8 × 0 =	8 × 1 =	8 × 10 =	2 × 10 =
p	9 × 0 =	9 × 1 =	9 × 10 =	1 × 1 =
q	10 × 0 =	10 × 1 =	10 × 10 =	10 × 0 =

r) What happens when you multiply any number by 0?

s) What happens when you multiply any number by 1?

t) What happens when you multiply any number by 10?

Name_____ Date_____

Lesson 1 Quiz

Solve each problem.

a 4 × 1 = ____ **b** 5 × 0 = ____ **c** 4 × 10 = ____ **d** 6 × 0 = ____

e 7 × 1 = ____ **f** 9 × 10 = ____ **g** 8 × 1 = ____ **h** 3 × 10 = ____

i 8 × 10 = ____ **j** 6 × 10 = ____

Write the letter to match related number sentences.

6 × 0 ____   **a** 0 + 0 + 0 + 0 + 0
8 × 1 ____   **b** 0 + 0 + 0 + 0 + 0 + 0 + 0 + 0 + 0
2 × 10 ____   **c** 1 + 1 + 1 + 1 + 1 + 1 + 1 + 1
9 × 0 ____   **d** 1 + 1 + 1
5 × 0 ____   **e** 0 + 0 + 0 + 0 + 0 + 0
3 × 1 ____   **f** 10 + 10
5 × 10 ____   **g** 10 + 10 + 10 + 10 + 10

These are the number facts I missed on the quiz:

Lesson 1: Multiply with 0, 1, and 10

LESSON 2

Multiply with 2

OBJECTIVES

Students will be introduced to the concept of multiplication as an array. Students will be able to solve repeated addition and master multiplication with 2.

DIRECT INSTRUCTION

Teach students that double addition facts (a number added to itself) are the same as multiplication by 2. Write on the board *0 + 0 = ?* Have students say the answer, and write it on the board. Then, show them how to change 0 + 0 = 0 into 2 x 0 = 0. Ask students how many zeroes are in 0 + 0 = ? After students answer 2 zeroes, show them that 2 x 0 = 0 says 2 zeroes are 0. Repeat this process for all problems in the two times tables (e.g., 1 + 1 = 2 x 1= 2, 2 + 2 = 2 x 2 = 4) up to 10 + 10 = 2 x 10 = 20. Explain that the rule of doubles is that 2 times some number means double the number.

Place 6 **blocks** on an **overhead projector** or draw them on the board to create an image of a 2-by-3 array. Discuss how the array can be seen as addition and multiplication. Introduce students to the term *ordering rule* (the commutative law). Ask a volunteer to make with blocks or draw on the board an array for 2 x 4. Ask a different volunteer to use the same blocks or drawing to show 4 x 2. Explain that 4 x 2 is the "ordering partner" for 2 x 4. Explain that the order of the numbers does not matter. They will still have the same answer (product).

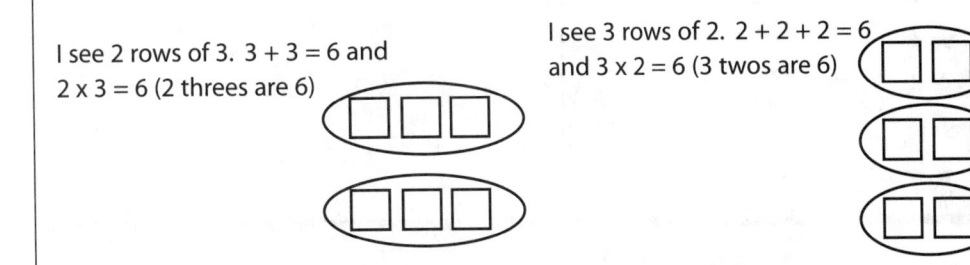

I see 2 rows of 3. 3 + 3 = 6 and 2 x 3 = 6 (2 threes are 6)

I see 3 rows of 2. 2 + 2 + 2 = 6 and 3 x 2 = 6 (3 twos are 6)

GUIDED PRACTICE

✓ Work with students in small groups to help them complete the **Ordering Rule reproducible (page 12).**

ASSESSMENT

✓ Have students complete the **Lesson 2 Quiz (page 13)** in 2 minutes. Challenge students to "beat their time" and complete the quiz in 1 minute and then again in 30 seconds to show that they have mastered the number facts.

Name_____   Date_____

Ordering Rule

Solve each problem.

a Write matching multiplication number sentences for the array. ★★★★★ ★★★★★ ____ × ____ = ____ ____ × ____ = ____	**b** Write matching multiplication number sentences for the array. ★★ ★★ ★★ ★★ ★★ ____ × ____ = ____ ____ × ____ = ____	**c** Write matching multiplication number sentences for the array. ★★★★★ ★★★★★ ____ × ____ = ____ ____ × ____ = ____
d Write matching multiplication number sentences for the array. ★★ ★★ ★★ ★★ ★★ ★★ ____ × ____ = ____ ____ × ____ = ____	**e** Draw an array for 2 × 4 = 8. (Draw X's)	**f** Draw an array for 4 × 2 = 8. (Draw X's)

Write the ordering partner for each multiplication fact.

g 2 × 1 = _2_ → _1_ × _2_ = _2_

h 2 × 0 = ____ → ____ × ____ = ____

i 7 × 2 = ____ → ____ × ____ = ____

j 2 × 10 = ____ → ____ × ____ = ____

k 2 × 9 = ____ → ____ × ____ = ____

l 2 × 2 = ____ → ____ × ____ = ____

m 3 × 2 = ____ → ____ × ____ = ____

n 2 × 8 = ____ → ____ × ____ = ____

o 6 × 2 = ____ → ____ × ____ = ____

p 2 × 4 = ____ → ____ × ____ = ____

q 5 × 2 = ____ → ____ × ____ = ____

r 0 × 2 = ____ → ____ × ____ = ____

Name_____   Date_____

Lesson 2 Quiz

Solve each problem.

- **a** 4 × 2 = ____
- **b** 1 × 2 = ____
- **c** 5 × 2 = ____
- **d** 6 × 2 = ____
- **e** 7 × 2 = ____
- **f** 9 × 2 = ____
- **g** 0 × 2 = ____
- **h** 3 × 2 = ____
- **i** 8 × 2 = ____
- **j** 10 × 2 = ____

Review Problems

- **k** 5 × 1 = ____
- **l** 9 × 0 = ____
- **m** 3 × 10 = ____
- **n** 6 × 0 = ____
- **o** 7 × 1 = ____
- **p** 1 × 0 = ____
- **q** 8 × 1 = ____
- **r** 2 × 2 = ____
- **s** 8 × 10 = ____
- **t** 6 × 10 = ____

These are the number facts I missed on the quiz:

LESSON 3

Multiply with 5

OBJECTIVES

Students will be introduced to multiplication of 5 using nickels and clock minutes. Students will master multiplication with 5.

DIRECT INSTRUCTION

Teach students that counting nickels is the same as multiplication with 5. Place 10 nickels on an **overhead projector.** Invite the class to count the nickels together (i.e., 5, 10, 15, . . . 50). Write on the board *2 x 5 = 10*. Ask the class how to read the multiplication problem, and wait for them to say *2 fives are 10*. Then, have volunteers use **overhead pens** to circle nickels to illustrate the multiplication problem. Erase students' circles, and repeat this process for each multiplication of 5 number sentence (i.e., 0 x 5 = 0 to 10 x 5 = 50).

Draw a clock on an **overhead transparency,** and have students draw one on **white paper** or on a **paper plate**. Use a **paper clip** as the minute hand on the clocks. Ask students to move their minute hand so it is pointing to the 1 on their clock. Invite the class to read the minutes (i.e., 5). Repeat this for each number on the clock. (Have students read the minutes as 60 when the minute hand points to 12.) Help students make the connection between reading the minutes on a clock and multiplying with 5. Explain to students that when they multiply a number on the clock by 5, they will find the number of minutes (e.g., multiply 6 by 5 to find 30 minutes).

GUIDED PRACTICE

✓ Have students work in small groups as you help them complete the **Nickels and Minutes reproducible (page 15).** Invite students to use **plastic coins** and the clock they made to help them.

ASSESSMENT

✓ Have students complete the **Lesson 3 Quiz (page 16)** in 2 minutes. Challenge students to "beat their time" and complete the quiz in 1 minute and then again in 30 seconds to show that they have mastered the number facts.

Name_____   Date_____

Nickels and Minutes

Write the value of the number of nickels.

# of nickels	1	2	3	4	5	6	7	8	9	10
Value of nickels	(1x5=?) ____?	(2x5=?) ____?	(3x5=?) ____?	(4x5=?) ____?	(5x5=?) ____?	(6x5=?) ____?	(7x5=?) ____?	(8x5=?) ____?	(9x5=?) ____?	(10x5=?) ____?

Write multiplication number sentences.

a 1 nickel: $\underline{1} \times \underline{5} = \underline{5}$ the ordering partner fact is $\underline{5} \times \underline{1} = \underline{5}$

b 2 nickels: ___ × ___ = ___   the ordering partner fact is ___ × ___ = ___

c 3 nickels: ___ × ___ = ___   the ordering partner fact is ___ × ___ = ___

d 4 nickels: ___ × ___ = ___   the ordering partner fact is ___ × ___ = ___

e 5 nickels: ___ × ___ = ___   the ordering partner fact is ___ × ___ = ___

f 6 nickels: ___ × ___ = ___   the ordering partner fact is ___ × ___ = ___

g 7 nickels: ___ × ___ = ___   the ordering partner fact is ___ × ___ = ___

h 8 nickels: ___ × ___ = ___   the ordering partner fact is ___ × ___ = ___

i 9 nickels: ___ × ___ = ___   the ordering partner fact is ___ × ___ = ___

j 10 nickels: ___ × ___ = ___   the ordering partner fact is ___ × ___ = ___

Create a multiplication sentence by writing × 5 in each box of the second row. Read the multiplication sentence down and write the answer in the bottom row. Your answer will tell you how many minutes past the hour it is when the minute hand points to a number on the clock. The first column is done as an example.

Minute hand is at (n)	1	3	6	9	4	5	7	8	10	11	12
(n) × 5	× 5										
How many minutes?	5 minutes	minutes	minutes	minutes	minutes	minutes	minutes	minutes	minutes	minutes	minutes

Lesson 3: Multiply with 5   15

Name_____ Date_____

Lesson 3 Quiz

Solve each problem.

a 2 × 5 = ____   **b** 1 × 5 = ____

c 3 × 5 = ____   **d** 4 × 5 = ____

e 7 × 5 = ____   **f** 9 × 5 = ____

g 8 × 5 = ____   **h** 6 × 5 = ____

i 5 × 5 = ____   **j** 10 × 5 = ____

Review Problems

k 2 × 2 = ____   **l** 8 × 2 = ____

m 5 × 2 = ____   **n** 4 × 2 = ____

o 10 × 1 = ____   **p** 9 × 2 = ____

q 7 × 2 = ____   **r** 6 × 0 = ____

s 0 × 5 = ____   **t** 0 × 1 = ____

These are the number facts I missed on the quiz:

Lesson 3: Multiply with 5

LESSON 4: Multiply with 9

OBJECTIVES

Students will be introduced to multiplication with 9 using patterns. Students will master multiplication with 9.

DIRECT INSTRUCTION

Make an **overhead transparency** of the **Shortcuts for the Nines reproducible (page 18),** and display it for the class. Use **white paper** to cover the bottom half of the page so only the "Pattern for the Nines" section is showing. Read aloud each multiplication problem, and then discuss with the class any patterns they see in the product. For example, the digits in the tens place are in order from 0 to 9 and the digits in the ones place are in reverse order from 9 to 0. Introduce the pattern described on the reproducible. Explain that the digit in the tens place is always one less than the number that is multiplied by 9 and that the sum of the digits in the tens place and the ones place always equal 9. Write on the board 8 x 9 = ? Write 7 in the tens place of the product because 7 is one less than 8. Ask the class what number should be written in the ones place of the product. (Remind them that the two digits must add up to 9.) Write 2 in the ones place, and say 8 x 9 = 72.

GUIDED PRACTICE

✓ Have students work in small groups as you help them complete the **Shortcuts for the Nines reproducible (page 18).**

ASSESSMENT

✓ Have students complete the **Lesson 4 Quiz (page 19)** in 3 minutes. Challenge students to "beat their time" and complete the quiz in 2 minutes and then in 1 minute (or less) to show that they have mastered the number facts.

Name_____   Date_____

Shortcuts for the Nines

Pattern for the Nines

1 × 9 = 09
2 × 9 = 18
3 × 9 = 27
4 × 9 = 36
5 × 9 = 45
6 × 9 = 54
7 × 9 = 63
8 × 9 = 72
9 × 9 = 81
10 × 9 = 90

Can you see this pattern?

*The digit in the tens place of the product is 1 less than the number multiplied by 9. This number plus the digit in the ones place will always equal 9.

Solve each problem.

a) 1 × 9 = ___	b) 10 × 9 = ___	c) 9 × 9 = ___
d) 5 × 9 = ___	e) 8 × 9 = ___	f) 2 × 9 = ___
g) 3 × 9 = ___	h) 6 × 9 = ___	i) 7 × 9 = ___
j) 0 × 9 = ___	k) 4 × 9 = ___	l) 9 × 5 = ___
m) 9 × 3 = ___	n) 9 × 1 = ___	o) 9 × 7 = ___
p) 9 × 5 = ___	q) 9 × 2 = ___	r) 9 × 10 = ___
s) 9 × 6 = ___	t) 9 × 0 = ___	u) 9 × 4 = ___

Lesson 4: Multiply with 9

Name_____   Date_____

Lesson 4 Quiz

Solve each problem.

a $2 \times 9 =$ ____   **b** $7 \times 9 =$ ____

c $8 \times 9 =$ ____   **d** $6 \times 9 =$ ____

e $1 \times 9 =$ ____   **f** $5 \times 9 =$ ____

g $4 \times 9 =$ ____   **h** $3 \times 9 =$ ____

i $10 \times 9 =$ ____   **j** $0 \times 9 =$ ____

Review Problems

k $5 \times 2 =$ ____   **l** $5 \times 5 =$ ____

m $3 \times 10 =$ ____   **n** $9 \times 9 =$ ____

o $7 \times 2 =$ ____   **p** $7 \times 1 =$ ____

q $8 \times 0 =$ ____   **r** $6 \times 1 =$ ____

s $9 \times 1 =$ ____   **t** $8 \times 10 =$ ____

These are the number facts I missed on the quiz:

Lesson 4: Multiply with 9

LESSON 5

Multiply with 4

OBJECTIVES

Students will be introduced to multiplication with 4 through the strategy of doubling twice (2 x 2n) and by using arrays. Students will master multiplication with 4.

DIRECT INSTRUCTION

Introduce students to multiplying with 4 by teaching them the strategy of doubling twice to find products (or doubling doubles). Write on the board *4 x 3 = ?* Tell students that one strategy for finding the product to this multiplication problem is to double twice. Write on the board *2 x 2n or (2 x n) + (2 x n)*. Explain that *n* is the number being multiplied by 4 (i.e., 3). Tell students they have to find 2n (i.e., 2 x 3 = 6), which is their first doubling. Then they have to find 2n again (i.e., 2 x 3 = 6), which is their second doubling. Tell them to add together the two products to find their product of 4 x 3. Write multiplication with 4 problems on the board from 0 x 4 to 10 x 4, and have students use the doubling twice strategy to find the products.

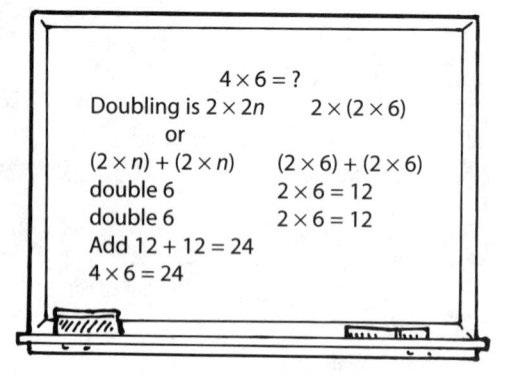

```
4 × 6 = ?
Doubling is 2 × 2n      2 × (2 × 6)
    or
(2 × n) + (2 × n)       (2 × 6) + (2 × 6)
double 6                2 × 6 = 12
double 6                2 × 6 = 12
Add 12 + 12 = 24
4 × 6 = 24
```

Have students practice drawing arrays to solve multiplication with 4. Draw on the board or an **overhead transparency** a large 10-by-10 grid. Write multiplication problems, and invite students to fill in the grid boxes to make arrays to help them determine the answer to each problem.

GUIDED PRACTICE

✓ Have students work in small groups as you help them complete the **Double Twice reproducible (page 21)**.

ASSESSMENT

✓ Have students complete the **Lesson 5 Quiz (page 22)** in 2 minutes. Challenge students to "beat their time" and complete the quiz in 1 minute and then again in 30 seconds to show that they have mastered the number facts.

Name_____   Date_____

Double Twice

Use the doubling doubles strategy to help you solve each multiplication problem. Circle the stars to illustrate each multiplication problem as shown in the example.

a
$2 \times 9 = 18$
$+$
$2 \times 9 = 18$

4×9 is double 9 twice = 36

b
$2 \times 8 =$
$+$
$2 \times 8 =$

4×8 is double ____ twice = ____

c
$2 \times 7 =$
$+$
$2 \times 7 =$

4×7 is double ____ twice = ____

d
$2 \times 6 =$
$+$
$2 \times 6 =$

4×6 is double ____ twice = ____

e
$2 \times 4 =$
$+$
$2 \times 4 =$

4×4 is double ____ twice = ____

f
$2 \times 3 =$
$+$
$2 \times 3 =$

4×3 is double ____ twice = ____

g
$2 \times 1 =$
$+$
$2 \times 1 =$

4×1 is double ____ twice = ____

h
$2 \times 10 =$
$+$
$2 \times 10 =$

4×10 is double ____ twice = ____

Name_____   Date_____

Lesson 5 Quiz

Solve each problem.

- **a** $1 \times 4 =$ ____
- **b** $5 \times 4 =$ ____
- **c** $7 \times 4 =$ ____
- **d** $6 \times 4 =$ ____
- **e** $10 \times 4 =$ ____
- **f** $8 \times 4 =$ ____
- **g** $0 \times 4 =$ ____
- **h** $4 \times 3 =$ ____
- **i** $4 \times 4 =$ ____
- **j** $9 \times 4 =$ ____

Review Problems

- **k** $2 \times 5 =$ ____
- **l** $4 \times 9 =$ ____
- **m** $3 \times 10 =$ ____
- **n** $5 \times 1 =$ ____
- **o** $4 \times 2 =$ ____
- **p** $6 \times 1 =$ ____
- **q** $8 \times 0 =$ ____
- **r** $7 \times 9 =$ ____
- **s** $4 \times 5 =$ ____
- **t** $9 \times 2 =$ ____

These are the number facts I missed on the quiz:

Lesson 5: Multiply with 4

LESSON 6

Multiply with 3

OBJECTIVES

Students will be introduced to multiplication with 3 by expanding on their knowledge of multiplication with 2. Students will master multiplication with 3.

DIRECT INSTRUCTION

Invite students to think of multiplication with 3 as an extension of multiplication with 2. Write on the board 4 x 3 = 4 x 2 + 4 = 12. Explain to students that multiplying with 3 is the same as multiplying with 2 and adding the number multiplied by 2 to the product. Write on the board multiplication problems beginning with 0 x 3 = ? and ending with 10 x 3 = ? Have the class help you find each product using the method of n x 2 + n.

Challenge students to solve more advanced multiplication problems by making them into simpler multiplication problems. Have students write the problem as an addition problem and multiply the ones column and write the product in the ones column of the answer. Then, have them multiply the tens column and write the product in the tens column of the answer. For example:

81 x 3 = ?	37 x 3 = ?
81 81 +81 3 × 8 = 24 → **24** 3 ← 3 × 1 = 3	37 37 +37 3 × 3 + 2 = 11 → **11** 1 ← 3 × 7 = 21
	Write the 1 in the ones column of the product and add the 2 to the product of the tens column.

GUIDED PRACTICE

✓ Have students work in small groups as you help them complete the **Connecting Times 3 to Times 2 reproducible (page 24)**.

ASSESSMENT

✓ Have students complete the **Lesson 6 Quiz (page 25)** in 2 minutes. Challenge students to "beat their time" and complete the quiz in 1 minute and then again in 30 seconds to show that they have mastered the number facts.

Name_____   Date_____

Connecting Times 3 to Times 2

Circle the stars to illustrate the problem. Write the product on the line.

a
★★
★★
★★   3 × 2 =

★★★
★★★
★★★   3 × 3 =

b
★★★★★★
★★★★★★   6 × 2 =

★★★★★★
★★★★★★
★★★★★★   6 × 3 =

c
★★★★★★★
★★★★★★★   7 × 2 =

★★★★★★★
★★★★★★★
★★★★★★★   7 × 3 =

d
★★★★★★★★
★★★★★★★★   8 × 2 =

★★★★★★★★
★★★★★★★★
★★★★★★★★   8 × 3 =

Use your multiplication knowledge to solve each problem.

a   31
       31
      +31
       93
      3×3 3×1

b   8
         8
        +8

c   70
        70
       +70

d   22
        22
       +22

e   11
        11
       +11

f   42
        42
       +42

g   53
        53
       +53

h   63
        63
       +63

i   16
        16
       +16

j   25
        25
       +25

24 Lesson 6: Multiply with 3

Name_____   Date_____

Lesson 6 Quiz

Solve each problem.

a $2 \times 3 =$ ____   **b** $1 \times 3 =$ ____

c $9 \times 3 =$ ____   **d** $4 \times 3 =$ ____

e $7 \times 3 =$ ____   **f** $5 \times 3 =$ ____

g $8 \times 3 =$ ____   **h** $6 \times 3 =$ ____

i $3 \times 3 =$ ____   **j** $10 \times 3 =$ ____

Review Problems

k $3 \times 0 =$ ____   **l** $3 \times 2 =$ ____

m $2 \times 9 =$ ____   **n** $7 \times 1 =$ ____

o $10 \times 4 =$ ____   **p** $5 \times 4 =$ ____

q $1 \times 1 =$ ____   **r** $9 \times 9 =$ ____

s $5 \times 5 =$ ____   **t** $8 \times 10 =$ ____

These are the number facts I missed on the quiz:

LESSON 7

Multiply with 6

OBJECTIVES

Students will be introduced to multiplication with 6 by expanding on their knowledge of multiplication with 5. Students will master multiplication with 6.

DIRECT INSTRUCTION

Invite students to think of multiplication with 6 as an extension of multiplication with 5. Write on the board *7 x 6 = 7 x 5 + 7 = 42*. Explain to students that multiplying with 6 is the same as multiplying with 5 and adding the number multiplied by 5 to the product. Write on the board multiplication problems beginning with *0 x 6 = ?* and ending with *10 x 6 = ?* Have the class help you find each product using the method of *n x 5 + n*.

Challenge students to solve more advanced multiplication problems by making them into simpler multiplication problems. Have students write the problem as an addition problem and multiply the ones column and write the product in the ones column of the answer. Then, have them multiply the tens column and write the product in the tens column of the answer. For example:

```
              60 x 6 = ?                                      73 x 6 = ?
                 60                                              73
                 60                                              73
                 60                                              73
                 60                                              73
                 60                                              73
                +60                                             +73
6 × 6 = 36 →    360    ← 6 × 0 = 0        6 × 7 + 1 = 43 →     43 8    ← 6 × 3 = 18
```

Write the 8 in the ones column of the product and add the 1 to the product of the tens column.

GUIDED PRACTICE

✓ Have students work in small groups as you help them complete the **Connecting Times 6 to Times 5 reproducible (page 27)**. Tell students to use the top row of coins (nickels) to help them solve problems times 5 and both rows of coins (nickels and pennies) to help them solve problems times 6. Challenge students to complete the bottom half of the reproducible independently.

ASSESSMENT

✓ Have students complete the **Lesson 7 Quiz (page 28)** in 2 minutes. Challenge students to "beat their time" and complete the quiz in 1 minute and then again in 30 seconds to show that they have mastered the number facts.

Name_____ Date_____

Connecting Times 6 to Times 5

Use the coins to help you solve each problem. Write the product on the line.

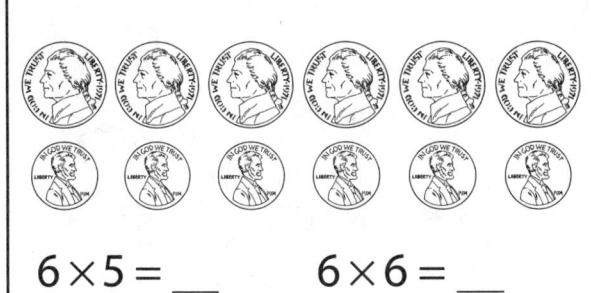

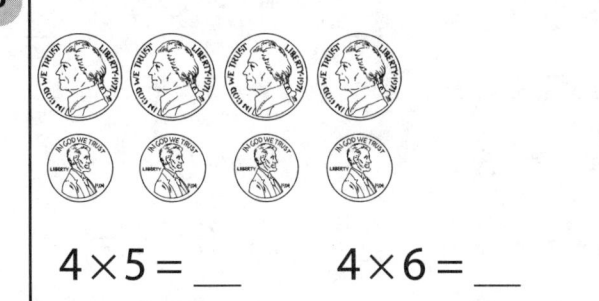

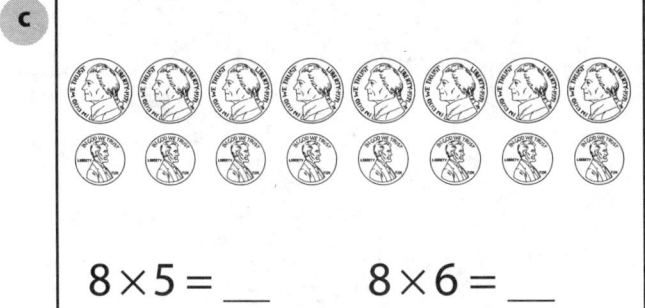

a
$6 \times 5 =$ __ $6 \times 6 =$ __

b
$4 \times 5 =$ __ $4 \times 6 =$ __

c
$8 \times 5 =$ __ $8 \times 6 =$ __

d
$2 \times 5 =$ __ $2 \times 6 =$ __

Use your multiplication knowledge to solve each problem.

e
```
   6
   6
   6
   6   6 × 6 = 36
   6
 + 6
  36
```

f
```
  11
  11
  11
  11
  11
 +11
```

g
```
  90
  90
  90
  90
  90
 +90
```

h
```
  50
  50
  50
  50
  50
 +50
```

i
```
  32
  32
  32
  32
  32
 +32
```

j
```
  85
  85
  85
  85
  85
 +85
```

k
```
  27
  27
  27
  27
  27
 +27
```

l
```
  16
  16
  16
  16
  16
 +16
```

Lesson 7: Multiply with 6

Name_____   Date_____

Lesson 7 Quiz

Solve each problem.

a 2 × 6 = ____   **b** 7 × 6 = ____

c 3 × 6 = ____   **d** 1 × 6 = ____

e 5 × 6 = ____   **f** 10 × 6 = ____

g 9 × 6 = ____   **h** 6 × 6 = ____

i 0 × 6 = ____   **j** 4 × 6 = ____

Review Problems

k 6 × 4 = ____   **l** 4 × 3 = ____

m 9 × 0 = ____   **n** 2 × 3 = ____

o 8 × 6 = ____   **p** 3 × 5 = ____

q 9 × 9 = ____   **r** 5 × 1 = ____

s 2 × 10 = ____   **t** 7 × 2 = ____

These are the number facts I missed on the quiz:

28 Lesson 7: Multiply with 6

LESSON 8

Multiply with 7 and 8

OBJECTIVES

Students will be introduced to multiplication with 7 and 8 using several strategies learned in previous lessons. Students will master multiplication with 7 and 8.

DIRECT INSTRUCTION

Introduce students to multiplication with 7 and 8 by writing all of the equations from 0 x 7 through 10 x 7 and 0 x 8 through 10 x 8 on an **overhead transparency** and displaying it for the class. Invite volunteers to solve each problem on the board using any strategy learned in lessons 1–7 (e.g., repeated addition, draw an array, expand on multiplication of 6). Have students explain how they found the product. Write the products on the overhead transparency. Invite the class to read through all of the equations after they have been solved correctly.

GUIDED PRACTICE

✓ Work with students in small groups to help them complete the **Practice Multiplying with 7 and 8 reproducible (page 30).**

ASSESSMENT

✓ Have students complete the **Lesson 8 Quiz (page 31)** in 2 minutes. Challenge students to "beat their time" and complete the quiz in 1 minute and then again in 30 seconds to show that they have mastered the number facts.

Name_____ Date_____

Practice Multiplying with 7 and 8

Write the letter to match related number sentences.

7 × 8 ____   a 8 + 8
3 × 7 ____   b 8 + 8 + 8 + 8 + 8 + 8 + 8
8 × 8 ____   c 7 + 7 + 7 + 7
4 × 7 ____   d 7 + 7 + 7 + 7 + 7 + 7 + 7 + 7
5 × 7 ____   e 8 + 8 + 8 + 8 + 8 + 8 + 8 + 8
2 × 8 ____   f 7 + 7 + 7 + 7 + 7
8 × 7 ____   g 7 + 7 + 7

Use your multiplication knowledge to solve each problem.

a	b	c	d
8 8 8 8 8 8 8 + 8 — 56 7 × 8	70 70 70 70 70 70 70 +70 —	61 61 61 61 61 61 61 +61 —	52 52 52 52 52 52 52 +52 —
e	f	g	h
96 96 96 96 96 96 96 +96 —	17 17 17 17 17 17 +17 —	83 83 83 83 83 83 83 +83 —	25 25 25 25 25 25 25 +25 —

Name_____   Date_____

Lesson 8 Quiz

Solve each problem.

a 2 × 8 = ____   **b** 8 × 8 = ____

c 9 × 7 = ____   **d** 7 × 7 = ____

e 6 × 7 = ____   **f** 7 × 8 = ____

g 3 × 8 = ____   **h** 3 × 7 = ____

i 1 × 8 = ____   **j** 4 × 7 = ____

Review Problems

k 3 × 1 = ____   **l** 8 × 5 = ____

m 6 × 6 = ____   **n** 8 × 4 = ____

o 7 × 5 = ____   **p** 8 × 9 = ____

q 4 × 3 = ____   **r** 10 × 0 = ____

s 4 × 2 = ____   **t** 9 × 4 = ____

These are the number facts I missed on the quiz:

Lesson 8: Multiply with 7 and 8   31

LESSON 9

Divide by 2 and 3

OBJECTIVES

Students will be introduced to division by 2 and 3.

Students will use the strategies of equally sharing and fact families to master division by 2 and 3.

DIRECT INSTRUCTION

Teach students that equally sharing something is the same as division. Gather **plastic coins** to help students understand this concept. Ask two volunteers to equally share two nickels. After each student takes one nickel, ask the students how much the nickels are worth together, how many coins there are, and how much money each student has. Write on the board *10 ÷ 2 = 5*. Repeat this with several volunteers with the following coin combinations: 15¢ (three nickels) ÷ 3, 40¢ (four dimes) ÷ 2, 50¢ (two quarters) ÷ 2, 75¢ (three quarters) ÷ 3, and 100¢ (four quarters) ÷ 2.

Introduce students to fact families. Write on the board *10 ÷ 2 = ?* Ask students to say the answer, and write it on the board. (Invite students to use coins to help them, if necessary.) Then, write *10 ÷ 5 = 2* and discuss its relationship to the previous division problem. Have students tell you the multiplication problems that are in this family (i.e., $5 \times 2 = 10$ and $2 \times 5 = 10$). Write additional division problems on the board, and have students help you write the fact family.

GUIDED PRACTICE

✓ Have students work in small groups as you help them complete the **Equal Sharing Division reproducible (page 33)**.

ASSESSMENT

✓ Have students complete the **Lesson 9 Quiz (page 34)** in 3 minutes. Challenge students to "beat their time" and complete the quiz in 2 minutes and then in 1 minute (or less) to show that they have mastered the number facts.

Name_____   Date_____

Equal Sharing Division

Read the sentence. Circle groups of coins to show division. Write a division number sentence and the answer to show how much money each person gets.

a

2 people equally share 12¢.

__12__ ÷ __2__ = __6__

Each person gets __6__ ¢.

b

3 people equally share 18¢.

____ ÷ ____ = ____

Each person gets ____ ¢.

c

2 people equally share 24¢.

____ ÷ ____ = ____

Each person gets ____ ¢.

d

3 people equally share 21¢.

____ ÷ ____ = ____

Each person gets ____ ¢.

e

2 people equally share 16¢.

____ ÷ ____ = ____

Each person gets ____ ¢.

f

3 people equally share 15¢.

____ ÷ ____ = ____

Each person gets ____ ¢.

Solve each problem and complete the number sentence. Use multiplication to check your answer.

g

2 people equally share 20¢. How much does each person get?

__20__ ÷ __2__ = __10__

Each person gets __10__ ¢.

2 people × __10__ ¢ = 20¢

h

3 people equally share 27¢. How much does each person get?

____ ÷ ____ = ____

Each person gets ____ ¢.

3 people × ____ ¢ = 27¢

i

2 people equally share 22¢. How much does each person get?

____ ÷ ____ = ____

Each person gets ____ ¢.

2 people × ____ ¢ = 22¢

Lesson 9: Divide by 2 and 3

Name_____ Date_____

Lesson 9 Quiz

Solve each problem.

a 15 ÷ 3 = ____   **b** 8 ÷ 2 = ____
c 12 ÷ 2 = ____   **d** 12 ÷ 3 = ____
e 18 ÷ 3 = ____   **f** 18 ÷ 2 = ____
g 27 ÷ 3 = ____   **h** 16 ÷ 2 = ____
i 14 ÷ 2 = ____   **j** 9 ÷ 3 = ____

Review Problems

k 4 × 4 = ____   **l** 8 × 3 = ____
m 7 × 2 = ____   **n** 7 × 3 = ____
o 6 × 6 = ____   **p** 8 × 8 = ____
q 5 × 8 = ____   **r** 4 × 7 = ____
s 9 × 3 = ____   **t** 4 × 3 = ____

These are the number facts I missed on the quiz:

34 Lesson 9: Divide by 2 and 3

LESSON 10

Divide by 4, 5, and 6

OBJECTIVES

Students will be introduced to the strategy of repeated subtraction to perform division by 4, 5, and 6.

Students will master division by 4, 5, and 6.

DIRECT INSTRUCTION

Teach students that repeated subtraction is a strategy they can use to help them solve a division problem. Gather **plastic coins** to help students visualize this strategy. Hold up four nickels, and write on the board *20 cents*. Ask the class to help you figure out how many times a person can take away 5 cents from 20 cents. Invite volunteers to each take away one nickel (5 cents) from the nickels you have. Each time a student takes a nickel, show the written form of this subtraction by subtracting 5 from the amount written on the board. Count how many students were able to take away a nickel, and explain that 5 can be subtracted from 20 four times and, therefore, 20 ÷ 5 = 4. Repeat this visual explanation for several division problems.

```
 20              18
- 5             - 6
 15   20 ÷ 5 = 4  12   18 ÷ 6 = 3
- 5             - 6
 10              6
- 5             - 6
  5              0
- 5
  0
```

GUIDED PRACTICE

✓ Give students play money and manipulatives.
✓ Have students work in small groups as you help them complete the **Repeated Subtraction and Equal Sharing reproducible (page 36)**.

ASSESSMENT

✓ Have students complete the **Lesson 10 Quiz (page 37)** in 3 minutes. Challenge students to "beat their time" and complete the quiz in 2 minutes and then in 1 minute (or less) to show that they have mastered the number facts.

Name_____ Date_____

Repeated Subtraction and Equal Sharing

Use repeated subtraction and equal sharing to solve each problem. Circle objects to help you share equally and show division.

---

a You want to make teams that each have 4 people on them. How many teams can you make with 20 people?

20 ÷ 4 = 5
5 teams
The answer is correct because
4 × 5 = 20.

b You want to keep 5 cats in each cage. How many cages do you need for 15 cats?

____ ÷ ____ = ____
____ cages
The answer is correct because
____ × ____ = ____.

c You want to put 4 fish in each bowl. How many bowls can you fill with 16 fish?

____ ÷ ____ = ____
____ bowls
The answer is correct because
____ × ____ = ____.

d You want to put 6 calculators in each box. How many boxes do you need for 30 calculators?

____ ÷ ____ = ____
____ boxes
The answer is correct because
____ × ____ = ____.

e You want to place 6 keys on each key ring. How many key rings do you need for 18 keys?

____ ÷ ____ = ____
____ key rings
The answer is correct because
____ × ____ = ____.

f You want to put 5 books on each shelf. How many shelves do you need for 30 books?

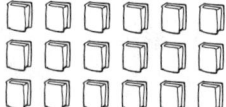

____ ÷ ____ = ____
____ shelves
The answer is correct because
____ × ____ = ____.

Use play money and manipulatives to help you solve each problem.

g You have $32.00. You spend $4.00 every day. How many days will your money last?

____ ÷ ____ = ____
____ days

The answer is correct because
____ days × $____ = $____.

h Your club has $42.00. 6 people will be sharing the money. How much money does each person get?

____ ÷ ____ = ____
Each person gets $____

The answer is correct because
____ people × $____ = $____.

i You have 40 apples. You eat 5 apples a day. How many days will the apples last?

____ ÷ ____ = ____
____ days

The answer is correct because
____ days × ____ apples = ____ apples.

Name_____ Date_____

Lesson 10 Quiz

Solve each problem.

a 8 ÷ 4 = ____   **b** 35 ÷ 5 = ____

c 24 ÷ 6 = ____   **d** 32 ÷ 4 = ____

e 15 ÷ 5 = ____   **f** 36 ÷ 6 = ____

g 20 ÷ 4 = ____   **h** 45 ÷ 5 = ____

i 48 ÷ 6 = ____   **j** 28 ÷ 4 = ____

Review Problems

k 10 × 4 = ____   **l** 8 × 5 = ____

m 7 × 3 = ____   **n** 0 × 2 = ____

o 8 × 8 = ____   **p** 9 × 2 = ____

q 8 × 9 = ____   **r** 7 × 1 = ____

s 9 × 6 = ____   **t** 4 × 4 = ____

These are the number facts I missed on the quiz:

Lesson 10: Divide by 4, 5, and 6

LESSON 11

Divide by 7, 8, and 9

OBJECTIVES

Students will use repeated subtraction and equal sharing to solve division problems. Students will master division by 7, 8, and 9.

DIRECT INSTRUCTION

Introduce students to division by 7, 8, and 9 by writing all of the equations (7 ÷ 7 through 7 ÷ 1, 8 ÷ 8 through 8 ÷ 1, and 9 ÷ 9 through 9 ÷ 1) on an **overhead transparency** and displaying it for the class. Invite volunteers to solve each problem on the board using the repeated subtraction or equal sharing strategy learned in lessons 9 and 10. Have students explain how they found the quotient. Write the quotients on the overhead transparency. Invite the class to read through all of the equations after they have been solved correctly.

GUIDED PRACTICE

✓ Give students **plastic or paper coins**. Have students work in small groups as you help them complete the **Dividing by 7, 8, and 9 reproducible (page 39)**.

ASSESSMENT

✓ Have students complete the **Lesson 11 Quiz (page 40)** in 3 minutes. Challenge students to "beat their time" and complete the quiz in 2 minutes and then in 1 minute (or less) to show that they have mastered the number facts.

Name_____ Date_____

Dividing by 7, 8, and 9

Use repeated subtraction or equal sharing to solve each problem.

a You want to put flowers in vases. You have 36 flowers and you can put 9 flowers in each vase. How many vases do you need?

_____ ÷ _____ = _____
_____ vases
The answer is correct because
_____ × _____ = _____.

b There are 14 birds in the tree. Each tree branch can hold 7 birds. What is the smallest number of branches needed for all of the birds to be able to sit on one tree?

_____ ÷ _____ = _____
_____ tree branches
The answer is correct because
_____ × _____ = _____.

c You are going river rafting with a group of 24 people. Each raft can have 8 people in it. How many rafts do you need for your trip?

_____ ÷ _____ = _____
_____ rafts
The answer is correct because
_____ × _____ = _____.

d Your grandma has 16 cats. Each bowl of food will feed 8 cats. How many bowls of food does she need to feed all of her cats?

_____ ÷ _____ = _____
_____ bowls of food
The answer is correct because
_____ × _____ = _____.

Use plastic or paper coins to help you solve each problem.

e There are 7 people in your house. You are going to equally share $42.00. How much money does each person get?

_____ ÷ _____ = _____
Each person gets $_____.
The answer is correct because
$_____ × _____ people = $_____.

f You have $64.00. You spend $8.00 every day. How many days will your money last?

_____ ÷ _____ = _____
_____ days
The answer is correct because
_____ days × $_____ = $_____.

g You have 72 baseball cards. You want to put the same number of cards in 9 envelopes. How many cards will you have in each envelope?

_____ ÷ _____ = _____
Each envelope will have _____ baseball cards.
The answer is correct because
_____ cards × _____ envelopes = _____ baseball cards.

Name_____   Date_____

Lesson 11 Quiz

Solve each problem.

a 7 ÷ 7 = ____	**b** 64 ÷ 8 = ____

c 56 ÷ 8 = ____	**d** 45 ÷ 9 = ____

e 54 ÷ 9 = ____	**f** 63 ÷ 7 = ____

g 80 ÷ 8 = ____	**h** 14 ÷ 7 = ____

i 48 ÷ 8 = ____	**j** 90 ÷ 9 = ____

Review Problems

k 18 ÷ 2 = ____	**l** 6 ÷ 3 = ____

m 12 ÷ 4 = ____	**n** 40 ÷ 5 = ____

o 36 ÷ 6 = ____	**p** 16 ÷ 2 = ____

q 27 ÷ 3 = ____	**r** 20 ÷ 4 = ____

s 35 ÷ 5 = ____	**t** 24 ÷ 6 = ____

These are the number facts I missed on the quiz:

LESSON 12

Mental Math and Multiples

OBJECTIVES

Students will be introduced to the concept of mental computation through the use of the distributive property and the generation of multiples. Students will show mastery of mental math and the use of multiples.

DIRECT INSTRUCTION

Teach students to perform multiplication in their head. Make an **overhead transparency** of the **Mental Multiplication reproducible (page 42),** and display it. Point to 2 x 20, and ask the class what it equals. Write the answer. Point to 2 x 25. Tell students that you will show them how to multiply this equation using mental computation. Point to the 2 and then point to the 2 in 25 and say *2 x 20 = 40*. Point to the 2 and then point to the 5 in 25 and say *2 x 5 = 10*. Explain that you will add these two products (40 + 10 = 50) to find the product of 2 x 25. Repeat this process for several problems. (This process uses the distributive property from left to right to help students perform mental computations.)

$2 \times 25 = ?$

$2 \times 20 = 40$
$2 \times 5 = 10$
$40 + 10 = 50$
$2 \times 25 = 50$

Discuss with the class what multiples are. Write on the board *Multiples are the products of two whole numbers*. Explain that the multiples of 2 are the products of 2 times another whole number. Have the class help you list the multiples of 2 (i.e., 2, 4, 6, 8, through infinity).

GUIDED PRACTICE

✓ Give each pair of students the **Mental Multiplication reproducible (page 42).** Invite students to take turns completing one problem at a time and explaining how they used mental math to solve it. Provide additional assistance to students who are having difficulty.

✓ Give each pair in a small group the **Mental Math Game (page 43).** Show students how to play the game with a volunteer as player B. Help students as they play, and assess their understanding of mental math.

INDEPENDENT PRACTICE

✓ Invite students to play with a partner the **Multiples Game (page 44).** Give each pair a **calculator** to check their answers.

✓ Give each student the **Problem Solving & Practice: Multiples and Mental Math reproducible (page 45)** to complete independently.

ASSESSMENT

✓ Have students complete the **Lesson 12 Quiz (page 46)** in 3 minutes. Challenge students to "beat their time" and complete the quiz in less time and then again in even less time to show that they have mastered this new concept.

Lesson 12: Mental Math and Multiples **41**

Name_____   Date_____

Mental Multiplication

Read each multiplication problem.

a	2 × 10 = ___	2 × 20 = ___	2 × 15 = ___	2 × 25 = ___	2 × 21 = ___
b	3 × 10 = ___	3 × 20 = ___	3 × 24 = ___	3 × 13 = ___	3 × 15 = ___
c	4 × 10 = ___	4 × 20 = ___	4 × 12 = ___	4 × 23 = ___	4 × 26 = ___
d	5 × 10 = ___	5 × 20 = ___	5 × 15 = ___	5 × 11 = ___	5 × 27 = ___
e	6 × 10 = ___	6 × 20 = ___	6 × 24 = ___	6 × 17 = ___	6 × 22 = ___
f	7 × 10 = ___	7 × 20 = ___	7 × 25 = ___	7 × 23 = ___	7 × 13 = ___
g	8 × 10 = ___	8 × 20 = ___	8 × 21 = ___	8 × 12 = ___	8 × 18 = ___
h	9 × 10 = ___	9 × 20 = ___	9 × 16 = ___	9 × 23 = ___	9 × 12 = ___
i	4 × 25 = ___	6 × 25 = ___	5 × 45 = ___	3 × 12 = ___	8 × 100 = ___

Lesson 12: Mental Math and Multiples

Mental Math Game

- Player A: Select any problem on the page, and write the answer under **Product A.**
- Player B: Write the answer you think is correct under **Product B.**
- Alternate turns until you have answered all of the problems.
- Use an answer key to determine which answers are correct.
- Circle the correct answers.
- Player A and Player B: Count how many answers you circled, and write that number for your points. The player with the most points is the winner.

Player A _____   Player B _____

Number Sentence	Product A	Product B	Number Sentence	Product A	Product B	Number Sentence	Product A	Product B
2 × 21 =			4 × 14 =			6 × 18 =		
2 × 25 =			4 × 22 =			6 × 33 =		
2 × 34 =			4 × 41 =			6 × 30 =		
2 × 42 =			4 × 11 =			7 × 41 =		
2 × 53 =			4 × 70 =			7 × 50 =		
2 × 57 =			4 × 32 =			7 × 13 =		
2 × 60 =			4 × 54 =			7 × 27 =		
2 × 38 =			5 × 42 =			7 × 18 =		
2 × 24 =			5 × 31 =			8 × 20 =		
2 × 14 =			5 × 25 =			8 × 14 =		
2 × 13 =			5 × 23 =			8 × 32 =		
3 × 22 =			5 × 15 =			8 × 17 =		
3 × 13 =			5 × 46 =			8 × 41 =		
3 × 30 =			5 × 20 =			9 × 13 =		
3 × 11 =			6 × 16 =			9 × 25 =		
3 × 31 =			6 × 22 =			9 × 42 =		
3 × 10 =			6 × 11 =			9 × 19 =		
3 × 16 =			6 × 26 =			9 × 36 =		
Points			**Points**			**Points**		

Players A's Total Points _____   **Players B's Total Points** _____

Multiples Game

- Player A: Select a number, circle it, and write the number under **Selected Number.**
- Try to write 9 multiples of that number (one in each box) next to the number.
- Count how many multiples you wrote, and record that number under **Player A's Points.**
- Player B: Repeat steps 1–3.
- Take turns and continue playing until there are no more numbers.
- Use a calculator to check your answers. The player with the most points is the winner.

Player A _____   Player B _____

2	3	4	5	6	7	8	9
10	11	20	30	70	90	60	70

Selected Number	Multiples	Player A's Points	Player B's Points

Total Points

Lesson 12: Mental Math and Multiples

Problem Solving & Practice: Multiples and Mental Math

Write a multiplication sentence to solve each problem. Draw a picture when needed.

a What numbers all have 18 as a multiple? (Hint: There are more than 2.)

b Write the first five multiples of 2 and 3. What is the smallest multiple that they share?

c Jamie has a sticker collection. She keeps 5 stickers in each bag. Bill has a baseball card collection. He keeps 6 cards in each bag. He has 5 bags. How many bags does Jamie have to have in order to have the same number of stickers as Bill's cards?

d What number has the following multiples: 6, 12, and 21?

Write the answer for each multiplication problem.

e 6 × 21 = _____
f 3 × 17 = _____
g 5 × 22 = _____
h 4 × 16 = _____
i 7 × 33 = _____
j 5 × 40 = _____
k 9 × 14 = _____
l 8 × 23 = _____
m 6 × 18 = _____
n 2 × 33 = _____
o 2 × 10 = _____
p 4 × 12 = _____
q 3 × 41 = _____
r 7 × 60 = _____
s 2 × 16 = _____

Name_____ Date_____

Lesson 12 Quiz

Use mental math to solve each problem.

a 6 × 14 = ____   **b** 7 × 21 = ____

c 8 × 61 = ____   **d** 9 × 41 = ____

e 5 × 42 = ____   **f** 7 × 51 = ____

List 5 multiples of each number.

g 8 ____ ____ ____ ____ ____

h 6 ____ ____ ____ ____ ____

i 5 ____ ____ ____ ____ ____

j 10 ____ ____ ____ ____ ____

These are the number facts I missed on the quiz:

Lesson 12: Mental Math and Multiples

LESSON 13

Prime and Composite Numbers

OBJECTIVES

Students will be introduced to prime and composite numbers. Students will show mastery of identifying prime and composite numbers.

DIRECT INSTRUCTION

Make an **overhead transparency** of the **Prime and Composite Numbers reproducible (page 48),** and copy a class set. Display the transparency, and give a reproducible to each student. Point out to students that the number 2 is circled and all of its multiples have an X drawn through them. Read all of the multiples. Ask students to circle the number 3 and draw an X through its multiples. Have the class repeat this for each number on the chart. List all of the numbers that are circled but are not crossed out (i.e., 2, 3, 5, 7, 11, 13, 17, 19, 23, 29, 31, 41, 61, 67, 71, 79, 83, 89, and 97). Explain to students that these numbers are prime numbers. Define a prime number as a number that only has 1 and itself as a factor (or is only divisible by 1 and itself). Explain that all of the numbers that are crossed out are called composite numbers.

GUIDED PRACTICE

✓ Give each student a new copy of the **Prime and Composite Numbers reproducible (page 48).** Invite students to repeat the steps listed above. Discuss each answer after all of the students have completed it. Provide additional assistance to students who are having difficulty.

✓ Have students work in small groups as you help them complete the **Is It Prime or Composite? reproducible (page 49).**

INDEPENDENT PRACTICE

✓ Invite students to play with a partner the **Prime or Composite Number Game (page 50).** (You may want students to use a calculator to add the factors.)

✓ Give each student the **Problem Solving & Practice: Prime and Composite Numbers reproducible (page 51)** to complete independently.

ASSESSMENT

✓ Have students complete the **Lesson 13 Quiz (page 52)** in 3 minutes. Challenge students to "beat their time" and complete the quiz in less time and then again in even less time to show that they have mastered this new concept.

Name_____   Date_____

Prime and Composite Numbers

~~1~~	②	3	~~4~~	5	~~6~~	7	~~8~~	9	~~10~~
11	~~12~~	13	~~14~~	15	~~16~~	17	~~18~~	19	~~20~~
21	~~22~~	23	~~24~~	25	~~26~~	27	~~28~~	29	~~30~~
31	~~32~~	33	~~34~~	35	~~36~~	37	~~38~~	39	~~40~~
41	~~42~~	43	~~44~~	45	~~46~~	47	~~48~~	49	~~50~~
51	~~52~~	53	~~54~~	55	~~56~~	57	~~58~~	59	~~60~~
61	~~62~~	63	~~64~~	65	~~66~~	67	~~68~~	69	~~70~~
71	~~72~~	73	~~74~~	75	~~76~~	77	~~78~~	79	~~80~~
81	~~82~~	83	~~84~~	85	~~86~~	87	~~88~~	89	~~90~~
91	~~92~~	93	~~94~~	95	~~96~~	97	~~98~~	99	~~100~~

List the prime numbers between 2 and 100.

_____

_____

48   Lesson 13: Prime and Composite Numbers

Name_____   Date_____

Is It Prime or Composite?

Look at the table below. The number 3 has an X under **Prime Number** because 3 only has itself and 1 as a factor. The number 4 has an X under **Composite Number** because 4 has other factors besides itself and 1. Draw an X under the correct heading for each number and explain why the number is prime or composite.

Number	Prime Number	Composite Number	Why is the number prime or composite?
3	X		3 × 1 = 3 and 3 has no other factors
4		X	2 × 2 = 4 and 1 × 4 = 4. 4 has 2 as a factor other than itself and 1
6			
7			
9			
11			
12			
13			
15			
16			
17			

Circle the correct answer.

a Which prime number is a factor of 12?
1   2   7   12

b Which prime number is a factor of 100?
5   10   20   50

c Which prime number is a factor of 20?
4   5   10   20

d Which prime number is a factor of 18?
3   6   5   14

e Which prime number is a factor of 21?
2   7   9   10

f Which prime number is a factor of 35?
4   6   7   30

g Which number is a multiple of 7?
10   12   14   20

h Which number is a multiple of 100?
150   200   230   310

i Which number is a multiple of 20?
4   5   15   40

Lesson 13: Prime and Composite Numbers   49

Prime or Composite Number Game

- **Player A:** Select a number, circle it, and write the number under **Selected Number**.
- Decide whether the number is prime or composite and draw an X in the correct column.
- Write all of the factors of the number. Add together the factors and record the sum under **Player A's Points**.
- **Player B:** Repeat steps 1–3.
- Take turns and continue playing until there are no more numbers.
- The player with the most points is the winner.

Player A _____   Player B _____

| 27 | 3 | 14 | 10 | 19 | 7 | 29 | 8 |
| 13 | 4 | 17 | 6 | 21 | 23 | 9 | 2 |

Selected Number	Prime	Composite	Factors	Player A's Points	Player B's Points
			Total Points		

Lesson 13: Prime and Composite Numbers

Name_____ Date_____

Problem Solving & Practice: Prime and Composite Numbers

Write a multiplication sentence to solve each problem. Draw a picture when needed.

a What number am I? I am a prime number. I am a factor of 15 and 30, but I am not a factor of 20.

b What number am I? I am a composite number. I have 2 and 4 as some of my factors. I have 24 as one of my multiples. I am not the number 8.

c What number am I? I am a composite number. The numbers 24 and 30 are a few of my multiples. The number 3 is one of my factors.

d What number am I? I am a prime number. I am greater than 20 but less than 40. I do not have a 3 as either of my digits.

Circle all of the composite numbers.

3   8   15   2   10   17   11   21   25   9   13   31

Circle all of the prime numbers.

1   5   12   19   6   29   33   14   2   7   4   24

Lesson 13: Prime and Composite Numbers 51

Name_____ Date_____

Lesson 13 Quiz

Circle the prime numbers.

3   5   7   9   11   13   15   17   19   21   23   25   27

Circle the correct answer.

a Which prime number is a factor of 12?

  1   3   7   12

b Which prime number is a factor of 20?

  5   10   20   40

c Which prime number is a factor of 50?

  4   5   10   20

d Which prime number is a factor of 18?

  3   6   5   20

e Which prime number is a factor of 21?

  2   7   9   10

f Which prime number is a factor of 28?

  4   6   7   56

LESSON 14

Multiply by Multiples of 10

DIRECT INSTRUCTION

Review basic multiplication facts with the class (one digit by one digit). Help students make the connection between multiplying by one-digit numbers and multiplying by multiples of 10 through the use of examples. Write the following examples on the board:

```
   12              12
×   2 tens     ×  20
  24 tens        240
```

Explain to students that they can think of the zeroes as placeholders in the ones place and, therefore, they can think 2 × 12 to solve the problem. Show them how to record the 0 in the answer as a placeholder and then multiply 2 × 2 and then 2 × 1. Write additional problems (e.g., 13 × 30, 22 × 10, 51 × 20) on the board, and have the class help you solve them.

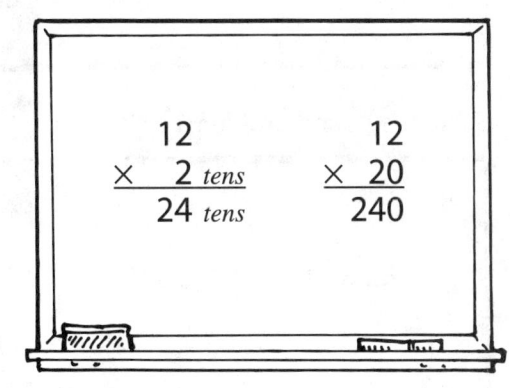

OBJECTIVES

Students will be introduced to the concept of multiplying by multiples of 10. Students will master the procedure for multiplying by multiples of 10.

GUIDED PRACTICE

✓ Give each student the **Multiplying by Multiples of 10 reproducible (page 54).** Complete the first one or two problems as a class. Invite students to complete one problem at a time, and discuss each answer after all of the students have completed it. Provide additional assistance to students who are having difficulty.

✓ Give each student the **More Multiples of 10 reproducible (page 55).** Complete the first one or two problems in the second section as a class. Have students work in small groups as you help them complete the remaining problems.

INDEPENDENT PRACTICE

✓ Invite students to play with a partner the **Multiples of 10 Product Game (page 56).** Give each pair a **calculator** to check their answers.

✓ Give each student the **Problem Solving & Practice: Multiples of 10 reproducible (page 57)** to complete independently.

ASSESSMENT

✓ Have students complete the **Lesson 14 Quiz (page 58)** in 10 minutes. Challenge students to "beat their time" and complete the quiz in less time and then again in even less time to show that they have mastered this new concept.

Lesson 14: Multiply by Multiples of 10   53

Name_____   Date_____

Multiplying by Multiples of 10

Example: The parade had 15 clowns in it. Each clown carried 20 balloons.
How many balloons were there altogether?

```
   15              15
×   2 tens      ×  20
   30 tens        300
```

Solve the paired problems.

a
```
   21        21
×   3     ×  30
```

b
```
   24        24
×   2     ×  20
```

c
```
   41        41
×   2     ×  20
```

d
```
   14        14
×   3     ×  30
```

e
```
   54        54
×   5     ×  50
```

f
```
   30        30
×   6     ×  60
```

g
```
   51        51
×   3     ×  30
```

h
```
   17        17
×   7     ×  70
```

i
```
   44        44
×   8     ×  80
```

Solve each problem.

a
```
   21
×  20
```

b
```
   27
×  30
```

c
```
   52
×  40
```

d
```
   31
×  20
```

e
```
   36
×  30
```

f
```
   26
×  20
```

g
```
   44
×  50
```

h
```
   26
×  60
```

i
```
   16
×  30
```

j
```
   20
×  40
```

Name_____   Date_____

More Multiples of 10

Solve each problem.

a) 91 × 20	b) 27 × 20	c) 71 × 20	d) 81 × 20	e) 64 × 20
f) 31 × 30	g) 61 × 30	h) 29 × 30	i) 65 × 30	j) 78 × 30
k) 31 × 40	l) 17 × 40	m) 72 × 40	n) 33 × 40	o) 15 × 40
p) 43 × 50	q) 87 × 50	r) 90 × 50	s) 32 × 50	t) 85 × 50

Solve the paired problems.

a) 213 × 2 213 × 20	b) 421 × 2 421 × 20
c) 131 × 6 131 × 60	d) 329 × 3 329 × 30
e) 640 × 5 640 × 50	f) 741 × 4 741 × 40
g) 207 × 9 207 × 90	h) 501 × 7 501 × 70

Lesson 14: Multiply by Multiples of 10   55

Multiples of 10 Product Game

- Player A: Select a number fact from the list, and draw an X over it.
- Write the fact under **Selected Number Fact**.
- Write the answer under **Player A Product**.
- Player B: Repeat steps 1–3.
- Take turns and continue playing until there are no more number facts.
- Use a calculator to check your answers.
- Add together all of your products to get your total points. The player with the most points is the winner.

Player A _____   **Player B** _____

41 × 50	42 × 20	53 × 60	71 × 60	35 × 50	52 × 40
92 × 40	84 × 50	22 × 40	60 × 70	52 × 80	64 × 60
79 × 40	24 × 40	46 × 20	68 × 80	53 × 30	37 × 70

Selected Number Fact	Player A Product	Player B Product

Total Points _____   _____

Lesson 14: Multiply by Multiples of 10

Name_____ Date_____

Problem Solving & Practice: Multiples of 10

Write a multiplication sentence to solve each problem. Draw a picture when needed. Use the back of this paper, if needed.

a It is Justin's birthday. There are 25 children at his party. Each child has 30 water balloons. How many water balloons are there in all?

b The town has 19 fire trucks. Each truck holds 50 gallons of gas. How many gallons of gas does it take to fill all 19 trucks?

c Mike collects football cards. He puts them into stacks of 12 cards each. He has 30 stacks of cards. How many cards has he collected?

d Jane sold popcorn at the school fair. Each bag had 90 pieces of popcorn in it. She sold 56 bags. How many pieces of popcorn did she sell?

Write the answer for each multiplication problem.

e 62 × 40

f 71 × 90

g 66 × 80

h 45 × 70

i 44 × 60

j 51 × 20

k 22 × 30

l 33 × 50

Lesson 14: Multiply by Multiples of 10   57

Name_____ Date_____

Lesson 14 Quiz

Solve each problem.

a) 32
  × 40

b) 51
  × 30

c) 62
  × 80

d) 49
  × 60

e) 45
  × 50

f) 61
  × 70

g) 21
  × 20

h) 74
  × 80

i) 16
  × 90

j) 53
  × 10

Review Problems

k) Which is a prime factor of 14?
   1   3   7   12

l) Which is a prime factor of 50?
   5   10   20   50

m) Which is a prime factor of 10?
   4   5   10   20

n) Which is a prime factor of 16?
   2   8   5   16

o) Which is a prime factor of 40?
   4   5   8   10

p) Which is a prime factor of 60?
   5   6   30   60

q) Which number is a multiple of 8?
   10   12   16   20

r) Which number is a multiple of 10?
   15   20   23   31

s) Which number is a multiple of 20?
   4   5   15   40

These are the number facts I missed on the quiz:

LESSON 15

Multiply by Two-Digit Numbers

OBJECTIVES

Students will be introduced to the concept of multiplying by two-digit numbers. Students will master the procedure for multiplying by two-digit numbers.

DIRECT INSTRUCTION

Students must show mastery in multiplying by multiples of 10 (lesson 14) to be able to perform multiplication by two-digit numbers. Review multiplying by multiples of 10 before teaching students this new concept.

$$\begin{array}{r} 25 \\ \times\ 12 \\ \hline \end{array} \qquad \begin{array}{r} 25 \\ \times\ 2 \\ \hline 50 \end{array} \qquad \begin{array}{r} 25 \\ \times\ 10 \\ \hline 250 \end{array} \qquad \begin{array}{r} 25 \\ \times\ 12 \\ \hline 50 \\ +\ 250 \\ \hline 300 \end{array}$$

Write the following word problem on the board: *There were 25 children in a field. Each child picked 12 flowers. How many flowers did the children pick altogether?* Ask students to help you write a multiplication equation to help you solve this problem. Write the following problem on the board:

$$\begin{array}{r} 25 \\ \times\ 12 \\ \hline \end{array}$$

Tell students that you will work together to break down the problem and make it easier to solve. Tell students you will first multiply 2 x 25 = 50. Then, multiply 10 x 25 = 250. Then, show students how to add these two products together to get 25 x 12 = 300. Repeat this process for several two-digit by two-digit multiplication problems.

GUIDED PRACTICE

✓ Have students work in small groups as you help them complete the **Multiplying by Two-Digit Numbers reproducible (page 60)**.
✓ Work with students in small groups to help them complete the **Practice with Two-Digit Numbers reproducible (page 61)**.

INDEPENDENT PRACTICE

✓ Invite students to play with a partner the **Two-Digit by Two-Digit Product Game (page 62)**. Invite students to use **scrap paper** to compute their products, and have students check each other's product using a **calculator**.
✓ Give each student the **Problem Solving & Practice: Two-Digit Numbers reproducible (page 63)** to complete independently.

ASSESSMENT

✓ Have students complete the **Lesson 15 Quiz (page 64)** in 10 minutes. Challenge students to "beat their time" and complete the quiz in less time and then again in even less time to show that they have mastered this new concept.

Multiplying by Two-Digit Numbers

Example: The class had 32 students in it. Each student had 24 stickers. How many stickers did they have altogether?

```
    32         32         32              32
   ×24        × 4    +   ×20       =     ×24
              128        640             128
                                        +640
                                         768
```

Solve each set of problems.

a
```
   32        32        32
 ×  1      × 20      × 21
```

b
```
   34        34        34
 ×  2      × 30      × 32
```

c
```
   42        42        42
 ×  3      × 20      × 23
```

d
```
   53        53        53
 ×  3      × 30      × 33
```

e
```
   52        52        52
 ×  1      × 40      × 41
```

f
```
   12        12        12
 ×  4      × 10      × 14
```

g
```
   72        72        72
 ×  2      × 20      × 22
```

h
```
   32        32        32
 ×  7      × 40      × 47
```

Name_____   Date_____

Practice with Two-Digit Numbers

Solve the problems.

a. 72 × 11	b. 32 × 21	c. 42 × 14	d. 72 × 25
e. 62 × 51	f. 42 × 21	g. 65 × 31	h. 60 × 51
i. 92 × 23	j. 90 × 13	k. 95 × 22	l. 42 × 43
m. 27 × 42	n. 37 × 12	o. 57 × 42	p. 63 × 52
q. 28 × 33	r. 48 × 30	s. 68 × 31	t. 54 × 35

Two-Digit by Two-Digit Product Game

- <u>Player A</u>: Select a number fact from the list, and draw an X over it.
- Write the fact under **Selected Number Fact**.
- Write the answer under **Player A Product**.
- <u>Player B</u>: Repeat steps 1–3.
- Take turns and continue playing until there are no more number facts.
- Use a calculator to check your partner's answers.
- Add together all of your products to get your total points. The player with the most points is the winner.

Player A _____ **Player B** _____

41 × 49	42 × 22	59 × 62	47 × 67	36 × 52	58 × 49
92 × 42	88 × 53	29 × 47	61 × 79	52 × 88	61 × 62
72 × 42	27 × 49	36 × 17	80 × 69	37 × 56	73 × 31

Selected Number Fact	Player A Product	Player B Product

Total Points _____ _____

Lesson 15: Multiply by Two-Digit Numbers

Name_____   Date_____

Problem Solving & Practice: Two-Digit Numbers

Write a multiplication sentence to solve each problem. Draw a picture when needed. Use the back of this paper, if needed.

a It is Beach Clean-Up Day. There are 25 people who picked up trash. Each person picked up 35 pieces of trash. How many pieces of trash did the people pick up altogether?

b Kevin and his family went to a parade. There were 19 elephants in the parade. Each elephant's assistant had a bag of peanuts to feed the elephant. Each bag had 45 peanuts in it. How many peanuts did the assistants have in all?

c Michelle has a large doll collection. She puts her dolls on shelves in her bedroom. She has 12 shelves with 37 dolls on each one. How many dolls does Michelle have in all?

d Write the missing numbers in the boxes.

a	21	20	22	24	25
b	630	600			750

What is the rule to find the missing numbers? Write the rule.

Write the answer for each multiplication problem.

e 73 × 22

f 64 × 23

g 55 × 24

h 97 × 26

i 37 × 22

j 44 × 63

k 86 × 27

l 75 × 51

Lesson 15: Multiply by Two-Digit Numbers 63

Name_____ Date_____

Lesson 15 Quiz

Solve each problem.

a) 53
× 22

b) 72
× 54

c) 81
× 26

d) 92
× 13

e) 58
× 26

f) 43
× 25

g) 70
× 38

h) 35
× 54

i) 96
× 47

j) 57
× 69

These are the number facts I missed on the quiz:

LESSON 16: Estimate Products Using Compatible Factors

OBJECTIVES

Students will be introduced to the concept of estimating products by using compatible factors to multiply. Students will master the concept of using compatible factors to estimate products.

DIRECT INSTRUCTION

Write the following problem on the board:

$$\begin{array}{r} 29 \\ \times\ 42 \end{array}$$

Explain to the class that they can substitute compatible factors (numbers close to the originals) to simplify this multiplication problem. Tell the class that rounding is one way to find compatible numbers. Write the following problem on the board:

$$\begin{array}{r} 30 \\ \times\ 40 \end{array}$$

Explain that you changed 29 to 30 because it is closer to 30 than 20 and you changed 42 to 40 because it is closer to 40 than 50. Have the class help you multiply the problem, and write the product (1,200). Point out that this estimated product is very close to the actual product of 1,218. Repeat this process for several problems. Use the sample problem below to show students how estimating products is helpful when multiplying money.

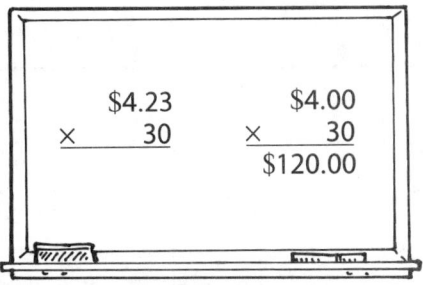

$$\begin{array}{r} \$4.23 \\ \times\ \ \ \ 30 \end{array} \qquad \begin{array}{r} \$4.00 \\ \times\ \ \ \ 30 \\ \hline \$120.00 \end{array}$$

GUIDED PRACTICE

✓ Have students work in small groups as you help them complete the **Estimating Products reproducible (page 66).** Provide additional assistance to students who are having difficulty.

✓ Give each pair in a small group the **Estimating by Compatible Factors reproducible (page 67).** Help students as needed, and assess their understanding as you observe them.

INDEPENDENT PRACTICE

✓ Invite students to play with a partner the **Estimate the Product Game (page 68).** Tell students to use **scrap paper** to compute their products, and have students check each other's product using a **calculator.**

✓ Give each student the **Problem Solving & Practice: Estimate Products reproducible (page 69)** to complete independently.

ASSESSMENT

✓ Have students complete the **Lesson 16 Quiz (page 70)** in 10 minutes. Challenge students to "beat their time" and complete the quiz in less time and then again in even less time to show that they have mastered this new concept.

Name_____   Date_____

Estimating Products

Estimate the product by using compatible factors to multiply.

Example: 26 × 23 → 30 × 20 = 600	**a** 41 × 18	**b** 48 × 18
c 62 × 22	**d** 43 × 11	**e** 56 × 18
f 771 × 17	**g** 451 × 81	**h** 576 × 48
i 424 × 28	**j** 345 × 33	**k** 502 × 28

Estimate by rounding each money problem to the nearest dollar.

| Example: 31 × $3.96 → 30 × 4 = $120 | **a** 48 × $5.17 | **b** 41 × $5.21 |
| **c** 21 × $9.07 | **d** 33 × $5.89 | **e** 43 × $7.77 |

Lesson 16: Estimate Products Using Compatible Factors

Names_____ Date_____

Estimating by Compatible Factors

Partners A and B: Take turns writing a compatible factor and then multiplying to find the estimated product.

Example 1:	Example 2:

46   50 *Partner A*
× 24 × 20 *Partner B*
       1,000 *Partner A*
	32 30 *Partner B*
	× 12 × 10 *Partner A*
	       300 *Partner B*

a
29
× 21

b
21
× 22

c
16
× 44

d
52
× 31

e
57
× 32

f
11
× 62

g
18
× 62

h
73
× 37

i
21
× 87

j
27
× 69

k
41
× 72

l
33
× 13

m
42
× 51

n
61
× 29

o
77
× 16

Lesson 16: Estimate Products Using Compatible Factors **67**

Estimate the Product Game

- Player A: Select a number fact from the list, and draw an X over it.
- Write the fact under **Selected Number Fact**.
- Write the answer under **Player A Product**.
- Player B: Repeat steps 1–3.
- Take turns and continue playing until there are no more number facts.
- Use a calculator to check your partner's answers.
- Add together all of your products to get your total points. The player with the most points is the winner.

Player A _____   **Player B** _____

41×49	42×22	59×62	47×67	16×66	58×49
92×42	88×53	33×23	61×79	52×12	21×62
72×42	27×49	58×11	84×69	37×56	73×31

Selected Number Fact	Player A Product	Player B Product

Total Points _____ _____

Lesson 16: Estimate Products Using Compatible Factors

Name_____   Date_____

Problem Solving & Practice: Estimate Products

Estimate to solve each problem. Draw a picture when needed.

a Bob went to the bookstore. There were 28 shelves of books. Each shelf held 31 books on it. Estimate how many books were in the bookstore.

b Tova's mom made cupcakes for her party. She made 47 cupcakes. Each cupcake had 19 sprinkles on it. About how many sprinkles did she use in all?

c Mark had a garage sale. He sold each poster for $1.90. Estimate how much money he made by selling 86 posters.

d Barby sold lemonade to her neighbors. She sold 81 cups of lemonade. Each cup cost $1.75. Estimate how much money she made selling lemonade.

Estimate by rounding each factor and then multiplying to find each product.

Example:

$$\begin{array}{r} 38 \\ \times\ 5.32 \end{array}$$

$$\begin{array}{r} 40 \\ \times\ \underline{5} \\ 200 \end{array}$$

e
$$\begin{array}{r} 42 \\ \times\ 2.97 \end{array}$$

f
$$\begin{array}{r} 38 \\ \times\ 8.23 \end{array}$$

g
$$\begin{array}{r} 326 \\ \times\ 6.17 \end{array}$$

h
$$\begin{array}{r} 437 \\ \times\ 3.27 \end{array}$$

i
$$\begin{array}{r} 543 \\ \times\ 2.17 \end{array}$$

Lesson 16: Estimate Products Using Compatible Factors

Name_____ Date_____

Lesson 16 Quiz

Estimate the product by using compatible factors to multiply.

Example:
```
   26       30
×  23    ×  20
           600
```

a
```
   51
×  18
```

b
```
   58
×  38
```

c
```
  801
×  18
```

d
```
  531
×  17
```

e
```
   96
×  58
```

Estimate by rounding each factor and then multiplying to find each product.

Example:
```
     13        10
×  5.65    ×   6
               60
```

a
```
     24
×  3.23
```

b
```
     56
×  2.79
```

c
```
     26
×  2.40
```

d
```
     37
×  8.11
```

e
```
     82
×  3.93
```

These are the number facts I missed on the quiz:

Lesson 16: Estimate Products Using Compatible Factors

LESSON 17

Divide Multiples of 10

OBJECTIVES

Students will be taught to connect division number facts to multiples of 10 using mental math. Students will show mastery in their ability to use mental math to perform division where the dividend is a multiple of 10.

DIRECT INSTRUCTION

Review the terms *dividend*, *divisor*, and *quotient* with the class, and remind students that dividend ÷ divisor = quotient. Use **paper or plastic money** (tens and hundreds) or have students create their own play money for this activity. Give a set of money to each student or small group. Have students use the money to solve problems at their desk as you solve them on the board. Write on the board *20 ÷ 2* and $2\overline{)20}$. Tape two $10 bills to the board, and tell the class you want to find out how much each person will get when you divide $20 between two people. Have the class solve the problem, and then repeat this activity with 400 ÷ 4, 120 ÷ 2, and 600 ÷ 2.

Discuss with the class the connection between sharing equally with the play money and solving the written number sentence. Write on the board *400 ÷ 2*, and show students 4 one-hundred-dollar bills. Ask the class how much each person would get when you divide $400 between two people. Show them that 400 ÷ 2 is the same as 4 hundreds ÷ 2 = 2 hundreds or 200. Explain that they can change a dividend that is a multiple of 10 into words (e.g., 4 hundreds) by removing the zeroes to simplify the problem and then divide to find the quotient. Repeat this process with several division problems.

GUIDED PRACTICE

✓ Give students **play money.** Have students work in small groups as you help them complete the **Divide Using Money reproducible (page 72).**
✓ Give students **play money.** Work with students in small groups to help them complete the **Divide Multiples of 10 reproducible (page 73).**

INDEPENDENT PRACTICE

✓ Invite students to play with a partner the **Multiples of 10 Quotient Game (page 74).**
✓ Give each student the **Problem Solving & Practice: Divide Multiples of 10 reproducible (page 75)** to complete independently.

ASSESSMENT

✓ Have students complete the **Lesson 17 Quiz (page 76)** in 10 minutes. Challenge students to "beat their time" and complete the quiz in less time and then again in even less time to show that they have mastered this new concept.

Name_____   Date_____

Divide Using Money

Use play money (tens and hundreds) to help you solve the problems.

Example:		
$2\overline{)4}$ quotient 2	$2\overline{)4\,tens}$ quotient 2 tens	$2\overline{)4\,hundreds}$ quotient 2 hundreds
$4 \div 2 = 2$	$40 \div 2 = 20$	$400 \div 2 = 200$

a

$3\overline{)6}$ $3\overline{)6\,tens}$ $3\overline{)6\,hundreds}$

$6 \div 3 =$ $60 \div 3 =$ $600 \div 3 =$

b

$4\overline{)8}$ $4\overline{)8\,tens}$ $4\overline{)8\,hundreds}$

$8 \div 4 =$ $80 \div 4 =$ $800 \div 4 =$

c

$5\overline{)25}$ $5\overline{)25\,tens}$ $5\overline{)25\,hundreds}$

$25 \div 5 =$ $250 \div 5 =$ $2500 \div 5 =$

d

$6\overline{)12}$ $6\overline{)12\,tens}$ $6\overline{)12\,hundreds}$

$12 \div 6 =$ $120 \div 6 =$ $1200 \div 6 =$

e

$8\overline{)32}$ $8\overline{)32\,tens}$ $8\overline{)32\,hundreds}$

$32 \div 8 =$ $320 \div 8 =$ $3200 \div 8 =$

Lesson 17: Divide Multiples of 10

Name_____   Date_____

Divide Multiples of 10

Solve each set of problems. Use play money to help you.

a	2)10	2)100 (10 *tens*)	2)1000 (10 *hundreds*)	b	2)14	2)140	2)1400
c	3)9	3)90	3)900	d	3)21	3)210	3)2100
e	4)16	4)160	4)1600	f	4)80	4)800	4)8000
g	5)50	5)500	5)5000	h	5)35	5)350	5)3500
i	6)36	6)360	6)3600	j	7)56	7)560	7)5600
k	8)72	8)720	8)7200	l	9)81	9)810	9)8100

Solve each set of problems.

m	n	o
20 ÷ 2 = ____	12 ÷ 3 = ____	14 ÷ 7 = ____
200 ÷ 2 = ____	120 ÷ 3 = ____	140 ÷ 7 = ____
2,000 ÷ 2 = ____	1,200 ÷ 3 = ____	1,400 ÷ 7 = ____
20,000 ÷ 2 = ____	12,000 ÷ 3 = ____	14,000 ÷ 7 = ____

Lesson 17: Divide Multiples of 10   73

Multiples of 10 Quotient Game

- Player A: Select a number fact from the list, and draw an X over it.
- Write the fact under **Selected Number Fact**.
- Write the answer under **Player A Quotient**.
- Player B: Repeat steps 1–3.
- Take turns and continue playing until there are no more number facts.
- Add together all of your quotients to get your total points. The player with the most points is the winner.

Player A _____ **Player B** _____

80 ÷ 2	640 ÷ 8	400 ÷ 5	120 ÷ 4	600 ÷ 2	350 ÷ 7
720 ÷ 9	630 ÷ 9	450 ÷ 5	200 ÷ 2	560 ÷ 8	240 ÷ 6
420 ÷ 7	320 ÷ 8	280 ÷ 4	270 ÷ 3	210 ÷ 7	300 ÷ 6

Selected Number Fact	Player A Quotient	Player B Quotient

Total Points _____

74 Lesson 17: Divide Multiples of 10

Name_____   Date_____

Problem Solving & Practice: Divide Multiples of 10

Use division to solve each problem. Draw a picture when needed.

a Don, Marc, Sarah, and Amy made $16,000 selling vegetables during the summer. How much money will each person get when they equally share the money?

b Mr. Locke and 5 other people won the lottery. The lottery was worth $36 million. When the money is equally divided, how much money will Mr. Locke receive?

c At the grocery store, the apples need to be stacked on flat trays. Each tray can hold 10 apples. There are 1,000 apples. How many trays are needed to stack all of the apples?

d The students at Ivanhoe School collected pencils to try to break a world record for the most pencils in one box. Each person collected 2 pencils. When they counted the pencils, they found that they had collected 6,000. How many students collected pencils?

Write the answer for each division problem.

e 3)150   **f** 5)50   **g** 7)560   **h** 8)640   **i** 6)420

j 6)180   **k** 2)60   **l** 9)450   **m** 4)120   **n** 7)280

Name_____   Date_____

Lesson 17 Quiz

Solve each problem.

a 3)‾120 = _____

b 5)‾250 = _____

c 7)‾280 = _____

d 8)‾320 = _____

e 6)‾540 = _____

f 2)‾400 = _____

g 6)‾600 = _____

h 9)‾360 = _____

i 4)‾200 = _____

j 7)‾350 = _____

These are the number facts I missed on the quiz:

Lesson 17: Divide Multiples of 10

LESSON 18

Divide by Tens

OBJECTIVES

Students will be introduced to division with a divisor that is a multiple of 10. Students will master division by multiples of 10.

DIRECT INSTRUCTION

Review dividing multiples of 10 (lesson 17) before teaching students to divide by multiples of 10. Use **paper or plastic money** (tens and hundreds) or have students create their own play money for this activity. Give a set of money to each student or small group. Have students use the money to solve problems at their desk as you solve them on the board. Show students the repeated subtraction method of division. Write on the board *Jon has $60.00 and he wants to spend $20.00 each day. How many days will his money last?* Tape 6 ten-dollar bills on the board. Repeatedly take away $20.00 until there is no money left (3 times). Show students the written form of this illustration: 60 − 20 = 40 − 20 = 20 − 20 = 0. Explain that the answer is the number of times 20 was subtracted. Repeat this process for several different word problems.

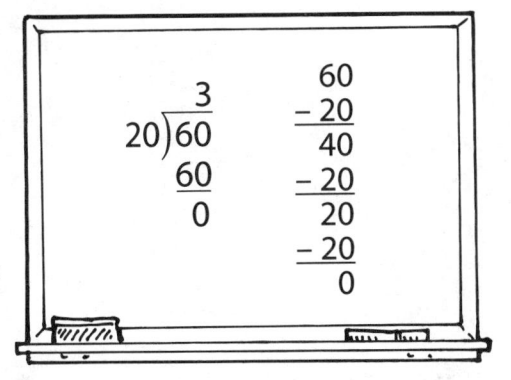

Tell students that when they are solving a division problem with a multiple of 10 as the divisor and the dividend, they can simplify the problem by crossing off a zero in both numbers. For example, they can think of 800 ÷ 20 as 80 ÷ 2, 100 ÷ 20 as 10 ÷ 2, and 200 ÷ 20 as 20 ÷ 2.

Write the following problems in pairs next to each other on the board:

$20\overline{)800}$ and $2\overline{)80}$ $20\overline{)100}$ and $2\overline{)10}$ $20\overline{)200}$ and $2\overline{)20}$

GUIDED PRACTICE

✓ Have students work in small groups as you help them complete the **Simplify Dividing by Tens reproducible (page 78)**.

✓ Work with students in small groups to help them complete the **Look at the Patterns reproducible (page 79)**.

INDEPENDENT PRACTICE

✓ Invite students to play with a partner the **Divide by Tens Quotient Game (page 80)**.

✓ Give each student the **Problem Solving & Practice: Divide by Tens reproducible (page 81)** to complete independently.

ASSESSMENT

✓ Have students complete the **Lesson 18 Quiz (page 82)** in 10 minutes. Challenge students to "beat their time" and complete the quiz in less time and then again in even less time to show that they have mastered this new concept.

Name_____   Date_____

Simplify Dividing by Tens

Example:

You have $100 and want to spend $20 each day. How many days will the money last? Look at the following methods you can use to solve this problem.

```
   100
 -  20
   80
 -  20
   60
 -  20
   40
 -  20
   20
 -  20
    0
```

$$20\overline{)100}$$ with 5 above, 100 below, remainder 0

$$2\overline{)10}$$ with 5 above

Solve each pair of problems.

a	b	c
2)8 20)80	3)60 30)600	4)40 40)400
d	**e**	**f**
2)140 20)1400	3)150 30)1500	4)120 40)1200
g	**h**	**i**
5)10 50)100	6)180 60)1800	7)280 70)2800
j	**k**	**l**
8)64 80)640	9)360 9)3600	2)16 20)160

78   Lesson 18: Divide by Tens

Name_____   Date_____

Look at the Patterns

Solve each set of problems and look at the patterns.

a	b	c
6)⎯6	5)⎯20	9)⎯72
60)⎯60	50)⎯200	90)⎯720
600)⎯600	500)⎯2,000	900)⎯7,200
6,000)⎯6,000	5,000)⎯20,000	9,000)⎯72,000

d	e	f
6 ÷ 2 = _____	12 ÷ 3 = _____	36 ÷ 4 = _____
60 ÷ 20 = _____	120 ÷ 30 = _____	360 ÷ 40 = _____
600 ÷ 200 = _____	1,200 ÷ 300 = _____	3,600 ÷ 400 = _____
6,000 ÷ 2,000 = _____	12,000 ÷ 3,000 = _____	36,000 ÷ 4,000 = _____

g	h	i
30 ÷ 6 = _____	35 ÷ 7 = _____	8)⎯640
300 ÷ 60 = _____	350 ÷ 70 = _____	80)⎯6,400
3,000 ÷ 600 = _____	3,500 ÷ 700 = _____	800)⎯64,000
30,000 ÷ 6,000 = _____	35,000 ÷ 7,000 = _____	8,000)⎯640,000

Lesson 18: Divide by Tens   **79**

Divide by Tens Quotient Game

- <u>Player A:</u> Select a number fact from the list, and draw an X over it.
- Write the fact under **Selected Number Fact.**
- Write the answer under **Player A Quotient.**
- <u>Player B:</u> Repeat steps 1–3.
- Take turns and continue playing until there are no more number facts.
- Add together all of your quotients to get your total points. The player with the most points is the winner.

Player A _____   **Player B** _____

120 ÷ 20	40 ÷ 20	150 ÷ 30	60 ÷ 30	250 ÷ 50	350 ÷ 50
280 ÷ 70	350 ÷ 70	210 ÷ 30	630 ÷ 30	800 ÷ 40	240 ÷ 60
810 ÷ 90	720 ÷ 80	320 ÷ 40	360 ÷ 60	120 ÷ 40	350 ÷ 10

Selected Number Fact	Player A Quotient	Player B Quotient

Total Points _____   _____

Name_____ Date_____

Problem Solving & Practice: Divide by Tens

Use division to solve each problem. Draw a picture when needed.

a. Dewey has $1200. He decides to give $200 to each of his friends. How many friends can he give $200?

b. Find the missing divisor. (Hint: There is no remainder.)

$$?\overline{)360} = 4$$

c. Colby has 2,000 baseball cards. He decides to give 50 cards to each of his friends. How many friends can he give cards?

d. Which number sentence has a quotient greater than 10?

A. 400 ÷ 40
B. 400 ÷ 200
C. 4000 ÷ 400
D. 400 ÷ 20

Write the answer for each division problem.

e. 20)140　**f.** 30)180　**g.** 50)400　**h.** 60)300　**i.** 30)900

j. 30)270　**k.** 60)180　**l.** 40)240　**m.** 60)360　**n.** 80)320

Lesson 18: Divide by Tens

Name_____ Date_____

Lesson 18 Quiz

Solve each problem.

a 20)140 = _____

b 30)150 = _____

c 50)300 = _____

d 60)240 = _____

e 70)350 = _____

f 80)160 = _____

g 90)810 = _____

h 40)840 = _____

i 60)840 = _____

j 70)490 = _____

Review Problems

k 6)120 = _____

l 6)360 = _____

m 9)360 = _____

n 4)400 = _____

o 7)420 = _____

These are the number facts I missed on the quiz:

Lesson 18: Divide by Tens

LESSON 19

Divide with Two-Digit Divisors

OBJECTIVES

Students will be introduced to division with two-digit divisors (that are not multiples of 10). Students will be taught to estimate the quotient and adjust the quotient if necessary. Students will master division of problems with a two-digit divisor.

DIRECT INSTRUCTION

Write the following problems on the board:
$19\overline{)170}$ and $20\overline{)170}$

Discuss with the class for which problem it is easier to estimate the quotient. Explain that it is easier to estimate the quotient of 170 ÷ 20 because 20 is a compatible number of 19. Remind students that a compatible number is a substitute number that is close to the original number and can be multiplied or divided easily. (Review Lesson 16: Estimate Products Using Compatible Factors, if necessary.) Show students how to solve this problem. Estimate the quotient for 170 ÷ 20 as 8 (20 x 8 = 160). Then, multiply the original divisor by the estimated quotient and solve the problem as shown below (problems in this lesson may have remainders). Repeat this process with several division problems using compatible numbers to replace the divisors.

Write the following problem on the board: $26\overline{)215}$
Have students estimate the quotient using the compatible number 30 to replace the divisor 26. The estimated quotient is 7 (30 x 7 = 210). Multiply the original divisor by the estimated quotient (26 x 7 = 182), and begin to solve the problem. When you subtract 182 from 215, students should notice that the remainder of 33 is larger than the divisor.

Use a compatible divisor. Estimate the quotient. Multiply the divisor by the estimated quotient and solve.

Explain that when the remainder is larger than the divisor, students will need to adjust their quotient by increasing it by 1 and then re-solve the problem. Tell students that if the product they get when they multiply the original divisor by the estimated quotient is larger than the dividend, they will need to adjust their quotient by decreasing it by 1 and then re-solve the problem.

GUIDED PRACTICE

✓ Have students work in small groups as you help them complete the **Compatible Divisors in Division reproducible (page 84)**.
✓ Work with students in small groups to help them complete the **Estimate & Adjust Your Quotient reproducible (page 85)**.

INDEPENDENT PRACTICE

✓ Invite groups of three students to play the **Quotient 4-in-a-Row Game (page 86)**. Have two students play the game while one student checks quotients using a **calculator**. Tell students to use **scrap paper** to compute their quotients.
✓ Give each student the **Problem Solving & Practice: Two-Digit Divisors reproducible (page 87)** to complete independently.

ASSESSMENT

✓ Have students complete the **Lesson 19 Quiz (page 88)** in 10 minutes. Challenge students to "beat their time" and complete the quiz in less time and then again in even less time to show that they have mastered this new concept.

Name_____   Date_____

Compatible Divisors in Division

When it is hard to estimate the quotient, use a compatible number for the divisor.

$29\overline{)153}$ $30\overline{)153}$ $3\overline{)15}^{5}$ $29\overline{)153}^{5R8}$
$\phantom{29\overline{)153}\quad 30\overline{)153}\quad 3\overline{)15}\quad}\underline{145}$
$\phantom{29\overline{)153}\quad 30\overline{)153}\quad 3\overline{)15}\quad 29\overline{)15}}8$

Step 1
Use a compatible divisor.

Step 2
Estimate the quotient.

Step 3
Multiply the divisor by the estimated quotient and solve.

Solve each problem using a compatible number for the divisor.

	Step 1	Step 2	Step 3
a	$48\overline{)113}$		
b	$58\overline{)426}$		
c	$79\overline{)401}$		
d	$59\overline{)241}$		
e	$42\overline{)89}$		

84 Lesson 19: Divide with Two-Digit Divisors

Name_____   Date_____

Estimate & Adjust Your Quotient

Sometimes, the compatible divisor method doesn't work. Then you have to adjust your quotient.

$21\overline{)161}$ $20\overline{)161}$ $2\overline{)16}^{\,8}$ $21\overline{)161}^{\,8}$ $21\overline{)161}^{\,7R14}$
                                                  $\underline{168}$ $\underline{147}$
                                                                         14

Step 1
Use a compatible divisor.

Step 2
Estimate the quotient.

Step 3
Multiply the divisor by the estimated quotient. Notice that the product 168 is bigger than the dividend 161.

Step 4
Adjust the quotient to 7 and solve.

Solve each problem using a compatible number for the divisor. Adjust your quotient when the remainder is bigger than the divisor (adjust up) or the product is bigger than the dividend (adjust down).

	Step 1	Step 2	Step 3
a	$46\overline{)240}$		
b	$33\overline{)296}$		
c	$27\overline{)168}$		
d	$63\overline{)310}$		
e	$24\overline{)153}$		

Lesson 19: Divide with Two-Digit Divisors   **85**

Quotient 4-in-a-Row Game

- Choose one player to be Player O, one player to be Player X, and one player to be the judge.
- <u>Player O:</u> Begin the game by choosing a problem and solving it. (Use compatible divisors to estimate the quotient. Some quotients may need to be adjusted. There are no remainders.)
- <u>Judge:</u> Use a calculator to check the quotient. If the quotient is correct, have Player O write an O in the box of the solved problem. If it is incorrect, have player X solve the problem and write an X in the box if the quotient is correct.
- Players take turns choosing and solving problems until one player correctly solves four problems in a row across, down, or on a diagonal.

Player O _____ **Player X** _____ **Judge** _____

a	$22\overline{)132}$	$41\overline{)82}$	$25\overline{)100}$	$21\overline{)147}$
b	$56\overline{)448}$	$36\overline{)108}$	$77\overline{)385}$	$24\overline{)168}$
c	$84\overline{)252}$	$32\overline{)192}$	$56\overline{)336}$	$27\overline{)135}$
d	$79\overline{)395}$	$34\overline{)102}$	$19\overline{)95}$	$63\overline{)378}$
e	$59\overline{)236}$	$44\overline{)88}$	$19\overline{)152}$	$23\overline{)161}$

Lesson 19: Divide with Two-Digit Divisors

Name_____ Date_____

Problem Solving & Practice: Two-Digit Divisors

Solve each problem. Draw a picture when needed.

a Which of the following will help you solve the equation 1000 ÷ 20?

A. 20 × 5000
B. 20 × 500
C. 20 × 50
D. 20 × 5

b Which of the following will help you solve the equation 3000 ÷ 20?

A. 20 × 1
B. 20 × 15
C. 20 × 150
D. 20 × 1500

c Find the missing digits in the division problem. (Hint: There is no remainder.)

4?) 378̄ with ? on top

d Find the missing digits in the division problem. (Hint: There is no remainder)

5?) 306̄ with ? on top

e Find the missing digits in the division problem. (Hint: There is no remainder.)

9?) 372̄ with ? on top

f Find the missing digits in the division problem. (Hint: There is no remainder.)

??) 1581̄ with 31 on top

Lesson 19: Divide with Two-Digit Divisors **87**

Name_____ Date_____

Lesson 19 Quiz

Solve each problem. Use compatible divisors to estimate the quotient. Quotients may need to be adjusted. (Hint: There are no remainders.)

a 52)156 = _____

b 54)432 = _____

c 56)504 = _____

d 51)153 = _____

e 57)399 = _____

f 62)124 = _____

g 63)630 = _____

h 65)260 = _____

i 68)748 = _____

j 69)552 = _____

These are the number facts I missed on the quiz:

LESSON 20

Square Numbers and Square Roots

OBJECTIVES

Students will be introduced to square numbers and square roots. Students will master finding square numbers and square roots and using the answers to perform multiplication and division.

DIRECT INSTRUCTION

Tell students that a square number is the product of any whole number times itself. Write on the board *1 x 1, 2 x 2, 3 x 3, 4 x 4, 5 x 5, 6 x 6, 7 x 7, 8 x 8, 9 x 9, 10 x 10,* and *11 x 11*. Next to each equation, write a new way of writing each problem (i.e., $1^2, 2^2, 3^2, 4^2, 5^2, 6^2, 7^2, 8^2, 9^2, 10^2$, and 11^2). Explain to students how to read 3^2 as *3 squared* or *3 to the second power*. Have students help you write the product to each problem, and explain that these products are square numbers. Write on the board the problems shown below, and have volunteers write the correct answers in the blanks.

$5^2 = \_ \times \_ = \_$ $20^2 = \_ \times \_ = \_$

$13^2 = \_ \times \_ = \_$ $30^2 = \_ \times \_ = \_$

$12^2 = \_ \times \_ = \_$ $40^2 = \_ \times \_ = \_$

Introduce square roots to the class. Write on the board $\sqrt{4}$, and explain that it is read as *the square root of 4*. Tell students that the answer to a square root is the number that when multiplied by itself equals the number shown inside the square root symbol. For example, the square root of 4 is 2 because 2 x 2 = 4. Write on the board $\sqrt{1}$, $\sqrt{36}$, $\sqrt{64}$, $\sqrt{25}$, $\sqrt{81}$, and $\sqrt{49}$, and have the class tell you the answers.

GUIDED PRACTICE

✓ Have students work in small groups as you help them complete the **Square Numbers reproducible (page 90)**. Make an **overhead transparency** of the reproducible, and give a copy to each student. Write 6^2 and color the squares on the grid. Have students color the square of each number from 1 to 10 on their paper as you assess their understanding. Provide help as needed.
✓ Work with students in small groups to help them complete the **Square Numbers & Square Roots reproducible (page 91)**.

INDEPENDENT PRACTICE

✓ Invite students to play with a partner the **Square Numbers & Roots Game (page 92)**.
✓ Give each student the **Problem Solving & Practice: Square Numbers & Roots reproducible (page 93)** to complete independently.

ASSESSMENT

✓ Have students complete the **Lesson 20 Quiz (page 94)** in 10 minutes. Challenge students to "beat their time" and complete the quiz in less time and then again in even less time to show that they have mastered this new concept.

Name_____ Date_____

Square Numbers

Color the squares for the following square numbers: $1^2, 2^2, 3^2, 4^2, 5^2, 6^2, 7^2, 8^2, 9^2$, and 10^2. Use a different color for each number. Label your answers.

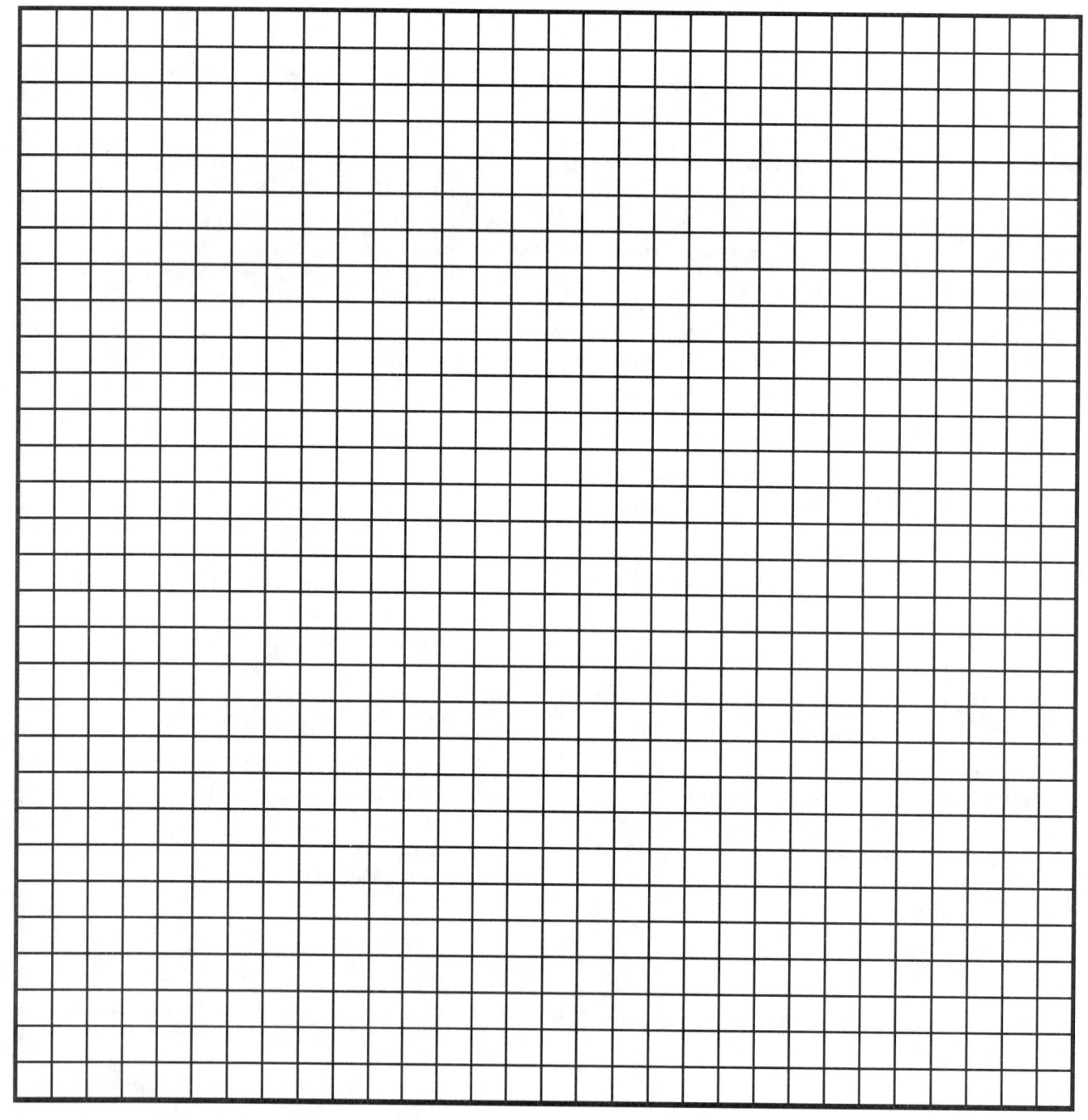

Name_____   Date_____

Square Numbers & Square Roots

6^2 is read as **6 squared** or **6 to the second power**. 6^2 means 6 × 6 = 36. $\sqrt{36}$ is read as **the square root of 36.** The square root of a number is the number that when multiplied by itself equals the given number. $\sqrt{36} = 6$.

Find the square numbers and the square roots.

Example: $5^2 = \underline{5} \times \underline{5} = \underline{25}$; $\sqrt{25} = \underline{5}$	a $4^2 = \underline{} \times \underline{} = \underline{}$; $\sqrt{16} = \underline{}$
b $0^2 = \underline{} \times \underline{} = \underline{}$; $\sqrt{0} = \underline{}$	c $10^2 = \underline{} \times \underline{} = \underline{}$; $\sqrt{100} = \underline{}$
d $3^2 = \underline{} \times \underline{} = \underline{}$; $\sqrt{9} = \underline{}$	e $9^2 = \underline{} \times \underline{} = \underline{}$; $\sqrt{81} = \underline{}$
f $8^2 = \underline{} \times \underline{} = \underline{}$; $\sqrt{64} = \underline{}$	g $7^2 = \underline{} \times \underline{} = \underline{}$; $\sqrt{49} = \underline{}$
h $6^2 = \underline{} \times \underline{} = \underline{}$; $\sqrt{36} = \underline{}$	i $12^2 = \underline{} \times \underline{} = \underline{}$; $\sqrt{144} = \underline{}$

Find the square numbers and square roots. Then use the answers to perform the given operation.

Example: $4^2 + 4 = (\underline{4} \overset{16}{\times} \underline{4}) + \underline{4} = \underline{20}$	j $5^2 + \sqrt{25} = (\underline{} \times \underline{}) + \underline{} = \underline{}$
k $0^2 \times \sqrt{25} = (\underline{} \times \underline{}) \times \underline{} = \underline{}$	l $\sqrt{100} \times 4^2 = \underline{} \times (\underline{} \times \underline{}) = \underline{}$
m $\sqrt{36} \times 2^2 = \underline{} \times (\underline{} \times \underline{}) = \underline{}$	n $\sqrt{81} + 5^2 = \underline{} + (\underline{} \times \underline{}) = \underline{}$
o $5^2 - \sqrt{25} = (\underline{} \times \underline{}) - \underline{} = \underline{}$	p $\sqrt{49} \times \sqrt{25} = \underline{} \times \underline{} = \underline{}$
q $\sqrt{100} + 5^2 = \underline{} + (\underline{} \times \underline{}) = \underline{}$	r $5^2 \times 2 = (\underline{} \times \underline{}) \times \underline{} = \underline{}$

Square Numbers & Roots Game

- **Player A:** Select any problem in the left column and write the answer under **Player A's Answer.** If the answer is correct, circle the answer.
- **Player B:** If the answer is not correct, write the answer under **Player B's Answer** and circle the answer if it is correct.
- Alternate turns and continue to play until you have completed all of the problems in the left column. Then play the right column.
- The winner is the player with the most correct answers (circled answers).

Player A _____   Player B _____

Problems	Player A's Answer	Player B's Answer	Problems	Player A's Answer	Player B's Answer
a) 10^2			b) $\sqrt{100} \times 2$		
c) $2^2 \times 2$			d) $\sqrt{64} \times 2$		
e) $4^2 + 2$			f) $\sqrt{25} \times 5$		
g) $4^2 - 6$			h) $\sqrt{36} \times \sqrt{36}$		
i) $10^2 - 50$			j) $\sqrt{25} - 5$		
k) $8^2 - 4$			l) $\sqrt{100} \times 5$		
m) $3^2 \times 2$			n) $\sqrt{64} \div 2$		
o) $9^2 + 9$			p) $\sqrt{9} + \sqrt{9}$		
q) $7^2 + 1$			r) $\sqrt{9} \times 3$		
s) $6^2 + 2$			t) $\sqrt{9} \times 4$		
u) $5^2 - 5^2$			v) $\sqrt{4} \times 4$		
w) $1^2 + 2^2$			x) $\sqrt{1} \times \sqrt{9}$		
y) $3^2 + 3^2$			z) $9 + \sqrt{9}$		
aa) $4^2 + 2^2$			bb) $\sqrt{9} \times \sqrt{4}$		
cc) $11^2 - 1$			dd) $\sqrt{81} \times 2$		
ee) 12^2			ff) $\sqrt{49} - 2$		
gg) $4^2 + 3^2$			hh) $\sqrt{25} \times \sqrt{25}$		
Points			Points		

Name_____   Date_____

Problem Solving & Practice: Square Numbers & Roots

Solve each problem. Show your work.

a There are 2 students who each have 8 pencils. How many pencils do they have in all? Write your answer as a square number.	**b** Max looked out his bedroom window. He saw 2 squirrels with acorns. The first squirrel had the same number of acorns as the square root of 64. The second squirrel had the same number of acorns as the square root of 16. How many acorns did the squirrels have altogether?
c Gabriella went for a walk on the beach to collect shells. The number of shells she collected is equal to 6 squared. How many shells did Gabriella collect in all?	**d** What number am I? You can find me if you find the square root of 25 and multiply it by the square root of 49 and then subtract 5.

Write the answer for each problem.

e $\sqrt{36} =$ _____   **f** $\sqrt{4} =$ _____

g $\sqrt{64} =$ _____   **h** $4^2 =$ _____

i $7^2 =$ _____   **j** $9^2 =$ _____

k $3^2 + 5^2 =$ _____   **l** $10^2 - 6^2 =$ _____

m $\sqrt{9} \times \sqrt{16} =$ _____   **n** $45 \div \sqrt{81} =$ _____

Lesson 20: Square Numbers and Square Roots

Name_____ Date_____

Lesson 20 Quiz

Solve each problem. Show your work.

Problem	Solution	Problem	Solution
a $10^2 + 4^2$		**b** $\sqrt{100} \div \sqrt{25}$	
c $2^2 + 6^2$		**d** $\sqrt{64} \times 2^2$	
e $3^2 + 2^2$		**f** $\sqrt{25} \times 5^2$	
g $4^2 - 2^2$		**h** $\sqrt{25} \times \sqrt{9}$	
i $10^2 + 5^2$		**j** $\sqrt{100} \times \sqrt{9}$	
k $8^2 - 6^2$		**l** $\sqrt{64} \div 2^2$	
m $4^2 \times 3^2$		**n** $\sqrt{9} \times \sqrt{9} \times \sqrt{9}$	
o $5^2 \times 3^2$		**p** $\sqrt{100} + \sqrt{9} + \sqrt{9}$	

These are the number facts I missed on the quiz:

Lesson 20: Square Numbers and Square Roots

Lesson 21: Least Common Multiple and Least Common Denominator

OBJECTIVES

Students will be introduced to the concept of finding the least common multiple (LCM) of a pair of numbers.

Students will be introduced to the concept of finding the least common denominator (LCD) to help them add and subtract fractions.

DIRECT INSTRUCTION

Review multiples with the class. Write the following story problem on the board: *At the amusement park, the roller coaster begins a new ride every 10 minutes and the rapids boat begins a new ride every 12 minutes. If they start at the same time, how many minutes later will they again start at the same time?* Show the class how to solve this problem by listing the multiples of 10 and the multiples of 12.

10: 10, 20, 30, 40, 50, <u>60</u>, 70, 80, 90, 100, 110, <u>120</u>
12: 12, 24, 36, 48, <u>60</u>, 72, 84, 96, 108, <u>120</u>

Show students that the common multiples of 10 and 12 are 60 and 120. Explain that the least common multiple or LCM is 60 and, therefore, the answer to the problem is that in 60 minutes, both of the rides will start at the same time. Repeat this process with other story problems.

Show students how to add fractions that have different denominators by finding the least common denominator or LCD. Write the following problem on the board:

$$\frac{1}{5} + \frac{3}{10}$$

Have students find the LCD. Tell students that the LCD is exactly the same as the LCM of 5 and 10. Since 10 is the LCD, they will have to make the denominator 5 into 10 by multiplying it by 2. Remind students that whatever they do to the bottom of a fraction they must also do to the top. Therefore, they must also multiply 1 by 2. The result will be the equivalent fraction of $\frac{2}{10}$. Have students solve the addition problem now that the denominators are the same.

$$\frac{1}{5} + \frac{3}{10} = \frac{1 \times 2}{5 \times 2} = \frac{2}{10} + \frac{3}{10} = \frac{5}{10} = \frac{1}{2}$$

GUIDED PRACTICE

✓ Have students work in small groups as you help them complete the **Least Common Multiples reproducible (page 96)**. Provide additional assistance to students who are having difficulty.

✓ Work with students in small groups to help them complete the **Least Common Denominator reproducible (page 97)**.

INDEPENDENT PRACTICE

✓ Invite students to play with a partner the **Fraction Game (page 98)**. Give a third player an answer key, and have him or her check answers.

✓ Give each student the **Problem Solving & Practice: LCM and LCD reproducible (page 99)** to complete independently.

ASSESSMENT

✓ Have students complete the **Lesson 21 Quiz (page 100)** in 10 minutes. Challenge students to "beat their time" and complete the quiz in less time and then again in even less time to show that they have mastered this new concept.

Name_____ Date_____

Least Common Multiples

Find the least common multiple (LCM) for each pair or set of numbers.

Example:	
4: 4, 8, ⑫, 16, 20 3: 3, 6, 9, ⑫, 15 LCM = 12	**a** 5: 10: LCM =
b 2: 10: LCM =	**c** 4: 6: LCM =
d 2: 6: LCM =	**e** 5: 6: LCM =
f 15: 10: LCM =	**g** 3: 6: LCM =
h 3: 9: LCM =	**i** 3: 12: LCM =
j 4: 10: LCM =	**k** 4: 5: LCM =
l 5: 15: LCM =	**m** 18: 6: LCM =
n 7: 21: LCM =	**o** 8: 12: LCM =
p 4: 8: 12: LCM =	**q** 4: 12: 24: LCM =

Least Common Denominator

Find the least common denominator (LCD) for each pair of fractions and solve the problem. Show your work.

Example: $\dfrac{1}{2} - \dfrac{3}{10} = \dfrac{1 \times 5}{2 \times 5} = \dfrac{5}{10} - \dfrac{3}{10} = \dfrac{2}{10} = \dfrac{1}{5}$	**a** $\dfrac{1}{5} - \dfrac{1}{10} =$
b $\dfrac{1}{8} + \dfrac{1}{2} =$	**c** $\dfrac{1}{2} - \dfrac{1}{10} =$
d $\dfrac{1}{6} - \dfrac{1}{12} =$	**e** $\dfrac{1}{20} + \dfrac{1}{10} =$
f $\dfrac{1}{15} + \dfrac{1}{30} =$	**g** $\dfrac{1}{50} - \dfrac{1}{100} =$
h $\dfrac{1}{6} - \dfrac{1}{18} =$	**i** $\dfrac{1}{30} + \dfrac{1}{10} =$
j $\dfrac{1}{5} + \dfrac{1}{25} =$	**k** $\dfrac{3}{5} - \dfrac{3}{10} =$
l $\dfrac{1}{12} - \dfrac{1}{18} =$	**m** $\dfrac{1}{9} + \dfrac{1}{27} =$
n $\dfrac{1}{15} + \dfrac{1}{5} =$	**o** $\dfrac{7}{25} - \dfrac{1}{10} =$
p $\dfrac{1}{5} - \dfrac{1}{100} =$	**q** $\dfrac{1}{100} + \dfrac{1}{10} =$

Lesson 21: Least Common Multiple and Least Common Denominator

Fraction Game

- The object of the game is to find the least common denominator (LCD) and solve the problem.
- Player A: Select any problem and compute the answer. If the answer is correct, you get a point.
- Player B: If Player A's answer is not correct, compute the answer. If your answer is correct, you get a point.
- Alternate turns and continue to play until you have completed all of the answers. The player with the most points is the winner.

Player A _____   Player B _____

		Player A's Points	Player B's Points
a	$\frac{1}{12} + \frac{1}{10} =$		
b	$\frac{1}{8} - \frac{1}{16} =$		
c	$\frac{1}{4} + \frac{1}{16} =$		
d	$\frac{2}{12} - \frac{1}{8} =$		
e	$\frac{1}{15} + \frac{1}{10} =$		
f	$\frac{1}{9} - \frac{1}{18} =$		
g	$\frac{1}{12} - \frac{1}{24} =$		
h	$\frac{1}{6} + \frac{1}{8} =$		
i	$\frac{3}{20} + \frac{1}{60} =$		
j	$\frac{1}{12} + \frac{1}{6} =$		
	Total Points		

Lesson 21: Least Common Multiple and Least Common Denominator

Name_____   Date_____

Problem Solving & Practice: LCM and LCD

Solve each problem. Show your work. Draw a picture when needed.

a The movie theater has two movies starting at 12:00 p.m. The first movie will last 2 hours and the second movie will last 3 hours. What is the next time that the two movies will begin at the same time?

b Tracks A and B are adjacent. One person runs on Track A and takes 4 minutes to go around. Another person runs on Track B and takes 6 minutes to go around. If the two runners start at a position that joins the two tracks, how many minutes later will they meet at the starting point? (Hint: Find the multiples of 4 and 6 to solve the problem.)

c Two dogs began to bury their bones. They buried their first bone in the same hole. The dog named Aussie buried each of his bones 3 feet apart. The dog named Magic buried each of her bones 4 feet apart. How many bones will each dog bury before they bury their bones in the same hole again?

Aussie:
Magic:

d Betty and Lucy are driving to Virginia. They both left at 5:00 p.m. Betty is driving 20 miles per hour and Lucy is driving 30 miles per hour. Lucy arrived at 7:00 p.m. What time will Betty arrive?

Find the least common multiple (LCM) of each pair of numbers.

e 2:
3:   LCM =

f 4:
7:   LCM =

g 3:
5:   LCM =

h 2:
9:   LCM =

Lesson 21: Least Common Multiple and Least Common Denominator

Name_____ Date_____

Lesson 21 Quiz

Find the least common multiple (LCM) for each pair of numbers.

a 3:
5: LCM =

b 4:
6: LCM =

c 8:
12: LCM =

d 3:
10: LCM =

e 45:
90: LCM =

Find the least common denominator (LCD) for each pair of fractions and solve the problem.

f $\dfrac{1}{12} + \dfrac{1}{8} =$

g $\dfrac{1}{8} - \dfrac{1}{20} =$

h $\dfrac{5}{6} + \dfrac{1}{8} =$

i $\dfrac{3}{20} + \dfrac{1}{15} =$

j $\dfrac{1}{12} + \dfrac{5}{6} =$

These are the number facts I missed on the quiz:

LESSON 22

Multiply with Decimals

DIRECT INSTRUCTION

Use **paper or plastic quarters** or have students create their own play money for this activity. Give a set of quarters to each student or small group. Have students use the coins to solve problems at their desk as you solve them on the board. Tape five quarters on the board, and have the class help you count them (i.e., 25¢, 50¢, 75¢, 100¢, 125¢). Convert counting quarters into multiplication by writing on the board *2 x 25¢, 3 x 25¢,* and so on. Rewrite 25¢ as 0.25 to introduce the class to multiplication with decimals ($\begin{smallmatrix}0.25\\\times2\end{smallmatrix}$), and show the class how they know where to put the decimal point in their product. Explain that they will count the total number of digits to the right of the decimal point(s) in the equation and place the decimal point in the answer that many digits from the right.

Show students repeated addition and multiplication with decimals to help them make the connection between adding and multiplying with decimals. Write on the board *A pizza costs $8.80. Jane bought 3.5 pizzas for her party. How much did she spend?* Show the class how to solve this problem using both repeated addition and multiplication. (Have them multiply decimals as whole numbers and place the decimal point in the product at the end.) Tell students to first multiply the price by 3 pizzas, then by 0.5 pizzas, and then show them how to find the answer for 3.5 pizzas.

1) $8.80
    × 3
    ─────
    $26.40

2) $8.80
    × 0.5
    ─────
    $4.400

3) $8.80
    × 3.5
    ─────
    4400
    26400
    ─────
    $30.800

    $8.80
    8.80
    + 8.80
    ──────
    $26.40

    half of $8.80
    is $4.40

    $26.40
    + 4.40
    ──────
    $30.80

OBJECTIVES

Students will be introduced to the concept of multiplying with decimals.

Students will master how to multiply with decimals and with money shown in decimal form.

GUIDED PRACTICE

✓ Have students work in small groups as you help them complete the **Multiplying with Money reproducible (page 102)**. Provide additional assistance to students who are having difficulty.

✓ Work with students in small groups to help them complete the **Multiplying Decimals by Decimals reproducible (page 103)**.

INDEPENDENT PRACTICE

✓ Invite students to play with a partner the **Multiplying Decimals Game (page 104)**.

✓ Give each student the **Problem Solving & Practice: Multiply with Decimals reproducible (page 105)** to complete independently.

ASSESSMENT

✓ Have students complete the **Lesson 22 Quiz (page 106)** in 10 minutes. Challenge students to "beat their time" and complete the quiz in less time and then again in even less time to show that they have mastered this new concept.

Name_____   Date_____

Multiplying with Money

Multiply the money in cents and in decimal form.

a	b	c	d
25¢ $0.25 × 2 × 2 ─── ─── 50¢ $0.50	25¢ $0.25 × 3 × 3 ─── ───	25¢ $0.25 × 4 × 4 ─── ───	25¢ $0.25 × 5 × 5 ─── ───
e 25¢ $0.25 × 6 × 6 ─── ───	**f** 25¢ $0.25 × 7 × 7 ─── ───	**g** 25¢ $0.25 × 8 × 8 ─── ───	**h** 25¢ $0.25 × 9 × 9 ─── ───
i 25¢ $0.25 ×10 × 10 ─── ───	**j** 25¢ $0.25 × 11 × 11 ─── ───	**k** 25¢ $0.25 ×12 × 12 ─── ───	**l** 25¢ $0.25 ×13 × 13 ─── ───

Solve each problem.

m $1.25 × 2	n $2.25 × 3	o $3.25 × 5	p $1.21 × 4	q $1.25 × 5
r $1.05 × 2	s $2.20 × 3	t $6.25 × 5	u $7.21 × 4	v $9.25 × 5
w $10.25 × 2	x $20.25 × 3	y $30.25 × 5	z $10.21 × 4	aa $100.25 × 5

Name_____   Date_____

Multiplying Decimals by Decimals

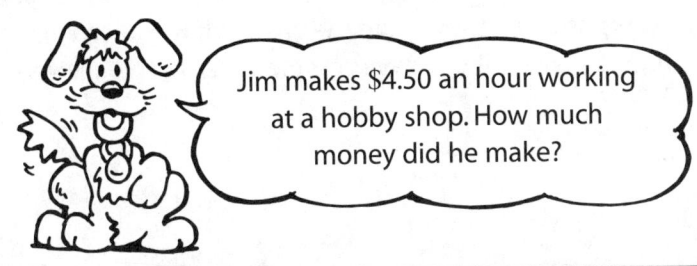

Jim makes $4.50 an hour working at a hobby shop. How much money did he make?

Jim worked 2 hours.	Jim worked 0.5 hour.	Jim worked 2.5 hours.
$4.50 × 2 $9.00	$4.50 × 0.5 $2.250	$4.50 × 2.5 2250 900 $11.250

The sum of the decimal places in the factors equals the decimal places in the product.

Solve each set of problems.

a
3.25   3.25   3.25
× 3   × 0.2 × 3.2

b
2.21   2.21   2.21
× 2   × 0.5 × 2.5

c
4.20   4.20   4.20
× 5   × 0.2 × 5.2

d
1.50   1.50   1.50
× 6   × 0.5 × 6.5

e
5.00   5.00   5.00
× 7   × 0.5 × 7.5

f
3.20   3.20   3.20
× 4   × 0.3 × 4.3

g
14.20 14.20 14.20
× 5   × 0.4 × 5.4

h
0.50   0.50   0.50
× 6   × 0.1 × 6.1

Lesson 22: Multiply with Decimals   103

Multiplying Decimals Game

- Player A: Select any problem and compute the answer. If the answer is correct, you get a point.
- Player B: If Player A's answer is not correct, compute the answer. If the answer is correct, you get a point.
- Alternate turns and continue to play until you have completed all of the answers. The player with the most points is the winner.

Player A _____   Player B _____

Problems	Player A's Points	Player B's Points	Problems	Player A's Points	Player B's Points	Problems	Player A's Points	Player B's Points
a) 0.25 × 4			b) 0.25 × 0.02			c) 2.50 × 0.01		
d) 0.36 × 2			e) 0.41 × 0.03			f) 8.92 × 10		
g) 3.12 × 4			h) 2.16 × 0.4			i) 8.92 × 0.1		
j) 5.41 × 7			k) 3.12 × 0.5			l) 7.25 × 0.03		
m) 4.25 × 3			n) 1.34 × 0.08			o) 5.25 × 5		
p) 6.25 × 6			q) 3.21 × 0.09			r) 8.12 × 0.2		
s) 5.72 × 4			t) 8.12 × 0.05			u) 3.22 × 9		
v) 4.12 × 2			w) 4.12 × 0.03			x) 4.75 × 3		
y) 8.81 × 5			z) 5.25 × 0.01			aa) 8.52 × 4		
Total Points								

Lesson 22: Multiply with Decimals

Name_____ Date_____

Problem Solving & Practice: Multiply with Decimals

Solve each problem. Show your work. Draw a picture when needed.

a The circus is in town. Adults' tickets cost $5.60 each. Children's tickets are half of the adult price ($2.80). What is the cost for 3 adults and 2 children to attend the circus?

b A city had 0.45 inch of rainfall every day for a week. How much rainfall did the city have during the entire week?

c Nikki's family traveled an average of 64.5 miles per hour for 8.5 hours. How many miles did her family travel altogether?

d During the summer, Shayna sold popcorn. On Sunday, she sold 10 bags. Each bag cost $1.75. How much money did she make selling popcorn?

e Maria bought a box of posters. She sold 200 of the posters for $1.90 each. How much money did she make selling the posters?

f Write the missing numbers in the boxes.

a	2.4	2.6	2.8	3.0	5.2
b	0.24	0.26			0.52

What is the rule to find the missing numbers? Write the rule.

Name_____ Date_____

Lesson 22 Quiz

Solve each problem.

a) 0.25 × 4

b) 0.25 × 8

c) 0.53 × 5

d) 0.41 × 9

e) 2.47 × 4

f) 2.7 × 0.1

g) 4.6 × 0.2

h) 3.4 × 0.3

i) 2.5 × 0.3

j) 8.3 × 0.5

k) 2.13 × 10

l) 5.14 × 100

m) 1.25 × 200

n) 6.21 × 30

o) 2.17 × 200

These are the number facts I missed on the quiz:

106   Lesson 22: Multiply with Decimals

LESSON 23

Sales Tax and Sale Price

OBJECTIVES

Students will be introduced to the calculation of sales tax and sale price with percents by multiplying decimals.

Students will master how to find sales tax and sale prices by multiplying decimals.

DIRECT INSTRUCTION

Discuss with the class what their local sales tax is (e.g., 6%) and what their experiences are with sales tax. Teach students how to convert sales tax (as a percent) into a fraction and into a decimal. Tell students that they can convert sales tax to a fraction by dropping the percent sign, writing the number over 100, and then reducing the fraction (6% = 6/100). Tell students that they can convert sales tax to a decimal by changing the percent sign to a decimal point and moving it two places to the left (6% = 0.06). Have the class convert 6.5%, 7%, and 7.5% sales tax to a fraction and to a decimal.

Teach the class how to calculate sales tax. Tell students you are buying a book for $16.00 and there is 6% sales tax. Explain that they need to multiply the cost of the book by the sales tax as a decimal ($16.00 x 0.06 = $0.96) to find the amount of tax you will pay. Explain that they would then add the sales tax to the cost of the book ($16.00 +$0.96 = $16.96) to find out the amount of their total purchase. Have the class find how much sales tax (e.g., 5%) they will pay on a purchase of $80, $20, $45, $12.60, and $15.40.

Show students how to calculate the sale price of an item. Tell them you are buying a stereo for $120.50 and it is on sale for 40% off the price. Explain that they can find the sale price in two ways. They can find the percent off by multiplying the price by 0.40 and subtracting the product from the price ($120.50 x 0.40 = $48.20; $120.50 – $48.20 = $72.30). Or, they can find what percent they will pay (60% because it is 40% off) by multiplying the price by 0.60 ($120.50 x 0.60 = $72.30).

GUIDED PRACTICE

✓ Have students work in small groups as you help them complete the **Sales Tax reproducible (page 108).** Provide additional assistance to students who are having difficulty.
✓ Work with students in small groups to help them complete the **Sale Price reproducible (page 109).**

INDEPENDENT PRACTICE

✓ Invite students to play with a partner the **Sales Tax Game (page 110).**
✓ Give each student the **Problem Solving & Practice: Sale Price & Tax reproducible (page 111)** to complete independently.

ASSESSMENT

✓ Have students complete the **Lesson 23 Quiz (page 112)** in 10 minutes. Challenge students to "beat their time" and complete the quiz in less time and then again in even less time to show that they have mastered this new concept.

Name_____ Date_____

Sales Tax

When you buy something, you pay sales tax. Sales tax varies depending on where you live. A sales tax of 5% means 5/100 or 0.05. A sales tax of 6% means 6/100 or 0.06. If you buy something for $60.00 and the sales tax is 6%, you multiply $60.00 x 0.06 = $3.60 to find the sales tax.

The sales tax is 5%. Compute the sales tax for each of the following purchases.

Example: $100 × 0.05 $5.00	**a** $50 × 0.05	**b** $200 × 0.05	**c** $400 × 0.05	**d** $1,000 × 0.05	**e** $4.80 × 0.05
f $60 × _____	**g** $600 × _____	**h** $40.90 × _____	**i** $5,000 × _____	**j** $480 × _____	**k** $30 × _____
l $10.50	**m** $64	**n** $48	**o** $9,000	**p** $40.50	**q** $30.40

The sales tax is 6%. Compute the sales tax for each of the following purchases.

Example: $10.53 × 0.06 $0.6318 Tax is $0.63.	**r** $50.50 × 0.06	**s** $200 × 0.06	**t** $400.50 × _____	**u** $1,000 × _____	**v** $4.80 × _____
w $60 × _____	**x** $600	**y** $40.90	**z** $5,000	**aa** $480	**bb** $30

Lesson 23: Sales Tax and Sale Price

Name_____   Date_____

Sale Price

When you buy an item that is on sale, you can find the sale price by multiplying the price of the item by the percentage off and subtracting the product from the price ($25 item x 0.20 discount = $5 off; $25 − $5 = $20 sale price). Or you can multiply the price of the item by the percentage you will be paying ($25 x 0.80 = $20).

Find the sale price of each of the following items.

20% off 80% of the price	40% off 60% of the price	10% off 90% of the price
Example: $200 $200.00 × 0.20 − 40.00 $40.00 $160.00 The sale price is $160.	$200 × 0.60 $120.00 The sale price is $120.	**a** $21 ×_____ The sale price is _____.
b $400 ×_____ The sale price is _____.	**c** $2.50 ×_____ The sale price is _____.	**d** $55 ×_____ The sale price is _____.
e $300 ×_____ The sale price is _____.	**f** $600.50 ×_____ The sale price is _____.	**g** $66 ×_____ The sale price is _____.
h $20 ×_____ The sale price is _____.	**i** $40.50 ×_____ The sale price is _____.	**j** $200 ×_____ The sale price is _____.
k $60 ×_____ The sale price is _____.	**l** $10.50 ×_____ The sale price is _____.	**m** $60 ×_____ The sale price is _____.
n $20.50 ×_____ The sale price is _____.	**o** $200.50 ×_____ The sale price is _____.	**p** $40 ×_____ The sale price is _____.

Lesson 23: Sales Tax and Sale Price   109

Sales Tax Game

- There are three games on this page. Play each column as a separate game.
- <u>Player A:</u> Select any problem in a column, compute the answer, and record it under **Player A**. If the answer is correct, circle it.
- <u>Player B:</u> If Player A's answer is not correct, compute the answer and record it under **Player B**. If the answer is correct, circle it.
- Alternate turns and continue to play until you have completed all of the answers. The player with the most points (circled answers) is the winner.

Player A _____   **Player B** _____

5% Sales Tax	Player A	Player B	6% Sales Tax	Player A	Player B	7% Sales Tax	Player A	Player B
a) 10 × 0.05			b) 200 ×			c) 40.50 ×		
d) 100 × 0.05			e) 400 ×			f) 10.50 ×		
g) 200 × 0.05			h) 300 ×			i) 8.80 ×		
j) 300 × 0.05			k) 20 ×			l) 4.40 ×		
m) 420 × 0.05			n) 60 ×			o) 8.20 ×		
p) 60 × 0.05			q) 20.50 ×			r) 21 ×		
s) 40 × 0.05			t) 200.50 ×			u) 55 ×		
Points:			Points:			Points:		

110   Lesson 23: Sales Tax and Sale Price

Name_____ Date_____

Problem Solving & Practice: Sale Price & Tax

Solve each problem. Draw a picture when needed.

a A toy costs $12.00 and the sales tax is 5%. How much will it cost to buy the toy, including sales tax? Show your work.

b A book costs $15. The sales tax is 6%. You have $15.50. Do you have enough money to buy the book? Explain your answer and show your work.

c A bicycle is on sale for 40% off the original price. The original price of the bicycle is $150. What is the sale price of the bicycle?

d What is the sales tax on an item that costs $120.99 when the sales tax rate is 6%?

A. $72.59
B. $0.72
C. $7.26
D. $725.94

e The price of a television is $100. It is on sale for 40% off. The sales tax is 7%. How much money will you pay to buy the TV, including sales tax? Show your work.

f The price of a shirt is $20.00. It is on sale for 20% off. The sales tax is 6%. How much money will you pay to buy the shirt, including sales tax? Show your work.

Lesson 23: Sales Tax and Sale Price   111

Name_____   Date_____

Lesson 23 Quiz

Solve each problem.

a Find the sales tax for a $300 purchase. The sales tax rate is 6%.

b Find the sales tax for a $15.50 purchase. The sales tax rate is 7%.

c Find the sales tax for a $1,000 purchase. The sales tax rate is 8%.

d Find the sale price of a bike. The sale price is 20% off the original price of $400.

e Find the sale price of a scooter. The sale price is 40% off the original price of $150.

f Find the sale price of a winter jacket. The sale price is 30% off the original price of $200.

Lesson 23: Sales Tax and Sale Price

Lesson 24: Estimate Percents Using Compatible Numbers

OBJECTIVES

Students will be introduced to the concept of estimating in percent problems using compatible numbers.

Students will show mastery in estimating percents using compatible numbers.

DIRECT INSTRUCTION

Discuss estimation with the class. Remind students that they can use compatible numbers (substitute numbers that are close to the original and can be multiplied easily) to estimate products. For example, 8 x 99 can be estimated as 8 x 100 = 800; 98 x 17 can be estimated as 100 x 17 = 1,700; and 6 x 197 can be estimated as 6 x 200 = 1,200. Show students that they can also use compatible numbers to estimate the answer to a percent problem. For example, 11% of 70 can be estimated as 10% of 70 or 0.1 x 70 = 7 and 24% of 40 can be estimated as 25% of 40 or 0.25 x 40 = 10.

GUIDED PRACTICE

✓ Have students work in small groups as you help them complete the **Estimation of Percents reproducible (page 114)**. Complete one problem at a time, and provide additional assistance to students who are having difficulty.

✓ Invite students to play with a partner the **Estimating Percents Game (page 115)**. As they play, walk around the classroom to help students and assess their understanding.

INDEPENDENT PRACTICE

✓ Invite groups of three students to play the **Estimate 4-in-a-Row Game (page 116)**. Two students will play while the third checks their products using a **calculator**. Tell students to use **scrap paper** to compute their products.

✓ Give each student the **Problem Solving & Practice: Estimate Percents reproducible (page 117)** to complete independently.

ASSESSMENT

✓ Have students complete the **Lesson 24 Quiz (page 118)** in 5 minutes. Challenge students to "beat their time" and complete the quiz in less time and then again in even less time to show that they have mastered this new concept.

Name_____ Date_____

Estimation of Percents

Estimate each answer using compatible numbers for the percents.

Example:	**a**	**b**	**c**	**d**
9% of 70 $\begin{array}{r}70\\\times\ 0.10\\\hline 7.00\end{array}$	24% of 99	29% of 70	19% of 70	21% of 70
e 24% of 72	**f** 18% of 100	**g** 18% of 99	**h** 19% of 100	**i** 21% of 200
j 92% of 101	**k** 79% of 100	**l** 11% of 307	**m** 12% of 810	**n** 46% of 210
o 92% of 300	**p** 93% of 400	**q** 11% of 607	**r** 52% of 610	**s** 46% of 510
t 9% of 85	**u** 48% of 97	**v** 18% of 40	**w** 19% of 89	**x** 18% of 685

114 Lesson 24: Estimate Percents Using Compatible Numbers

Estimating Percents Game

- Play each column as a separate game.
- Player A: Select any problem in a column and compute the answer. If the answer is correct, circle it.
- Player B: If Player A's answer is not correct, compute the answer. If the answer is correct, circle it.
- Alternate turns and continue to play until you have completed all of the answers. The player with the most points (circled answers) is the winner.

Player A _____   Player B _____

Estimate Using Compatible Numbers	Player A	Player B	Estimate Using Compatible Numbers	Player A	Player B
a. 9% of 103			k. 24% of 40		
b. 29% of 20			l. 24% of 301		
c. 19% of 33			m. 15% of 401		
d. 51% of 503			n. 9% of 21		
e. 99% of 302			o. 11% of 601		
f. 19% of 603			p. 24% of 70		
g. 77% of 397			q. 49% of 391		
h. 10% of 703			r. 11% of 905		
i. 28% of 305			s. 24% of 491		
j. 12% of 811			t. 97% of 152		
Points:			Points:		

Lesson 24: Estimate Percents Using Compatible Numbers   115

Estimate 4-in-a-Row Game

- Choose one player to be Player O, one player to be Player X, and one player to be the judge.
- Player O: Begin the game by choosing a problem and solving it. You may estimate using compatible numbers for the percents.
- Judge: Use a calculator to check the product. If the product is correct, have Player O write an O in the box of the solved problem.
- Player X: If Player O's answer is not correct, solve the problem. Write an X in the box if the product is correct.
- Take turns and continue playing until a player correctly solves four problems in a row across, down, or on a diagonal.

Player O _____ Player X _____ Judge _____

9% of 40	11% of 99	19% of 99	13% of 810
9% of 93	24% of 95	49% of 310	98% of 303
22% of 707	77% of 100	22% of 47	39% of 18
62% of 335	6% of 24	13% of 68	20% of 312
25% of 125	24% of 401	19% of 203	51% of 51

Lesson 24: Estimate Percents Using Compatible Numbers

Name_____ Date_____

Problem Solving & Practice: Estimate Percents

Use the information in the Table of Population to solve each problem. Estimate the answers using compatible numbers for the percents.

Table of Population (2002 Census)

Mega Cities of the World	Population (rounded)
Tokyo	26,000,000
Mexico City	19,000,000
Bombay	18,000,000
São Paulo	18,000,000
Shanghai	17,000,000
New York	17,000,000

9% of population is under 6 years old

22% of population is between 6 and 19

39% of population is between 20 and 50

21% of population is between 51 and 65

9% of population is 65 or older

---

a. About how many children under 6 years old live in Tokyo?

b. About how many children under 6 years old live in New York?

c. About how many people older than 65 years of age live in Mexico City?

d. About how many people between the ages of 20 and 50 live in New York?

e. About how many people between the ages of 20 and 50 live in Bombay?

f. About how many more people between the ages of 20 and 50 live in Bombay than live in New York?

g. About how many people between the ages of 51 and 65 live in Shanghai?

h. About how many people between the ages of 51 and 65 live in São Paulo?

i. About how many more people between the ages of 51 and 65 live in São Paulo than live in Shanghai?

Lesson 24: Estimate Percents Using Compatible Numbers 117

Name_____   Date_____

Lesson 24 Quiz

Estimate each answer using compatible numbers for the percents. Show your work.

a 87% of 300

b 14% of 400

c 11% of 600

d 51% of 610

e 49% of 510

f 9% of 80

g 9% of 60

h 11% of 100

i 18% of 810

j 19% of 90

These are the number facts I missed on the quiz:

118   Lesson 24: Estimate Percents Using Compatible Numbers

Lesson 25: Prime Factorization

OBJECTIVES

Students will be introduced to the concept of prime factorization. Students will show mastery in finding the prime factors of a composite number.

DIRECT INSTRUCTION

Discuss with the class how one number can be expressed as the product of several different pairs of factors (e.g., 12 can be expressed as the product of 3 x 4, 1 x 12, and 2 x 6). Write on the board the numbers 3, 10, 20, and 24. Have the class help you list the pairs of factors for each of these products. Explain that the number 3 is a prime number because it only has 1 and itself as factors and that the other numbers are composite numbers because they have additional factors. Review which numbers are prime with the class (see lesson 13).

Introduce factor trees to the class. Write the product 24 on the board, and ask the class to list its factor pairs. Draw a factor tree as shown below for each factor pair (omit 1 x 24), and write a multiplication sentence showing 24 as a product of its prime factors (its prime factorization). Explain that you need to continue to list the factors for each number until only its prime factors remain (usually 2, 3, 5, or 7). Point out that you get the same product regardless of the order of the factors in the multiplication sentence (associative property). Draw factor trees for several products.

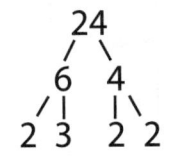

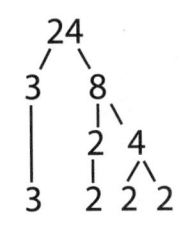

```
      24                              24
     /  \                            /  \
    6    4         or               3    8
   /|    |\                         |    |\
  2 3   2 2                         |   2  4
                                    |      /\
                                    3   2 2 2
```

$24 = 2 \times 3 \times 2 \times 2$ $24 = 3 \times 2 \times 2 \times 2$

GUIDED PRACTICE

✓ Have students work in small groups as you help them complete the **Factor Tree reproducible (page 120)**.
✓ Work with pairs of students to help them play the **Factors and Product Game (page 121)**.

INDEPENDENT PRACTICE

✓ Invite students to play with a partner the **Prime Factor Game (page 122)**. Have students draw factor trees on scrap paper.
✓ Give each student the **Problem Solving & Practice: Factors reproducible (page 123)** to complete independently.

ASSESSMENT

✓ Have students complete the **Lesson 25 Quiz (page 124)** in 10 minutes. Challenge students to "beat their time" and complete the quiz in less time and then again in even less time to show that they have mastered this new concept.

Name_____   Date_____

Factor Tree

A composite number can be written as the product of prime factors such as 10 = 2 x 5. 2 and 5 are prime factors of 10. To find the prime factors of a composite number, draw a factor tree. Then write a number sentence to show the composite number as the product of its prime factors. Finally, list the prime factors.

| Example:<br>```
      72
     /  \
    8    9
   /|\  / \
  2 4  3  3
   / \
  2   2
```<br>72 = 2 x 2 x 2 x 3 x 3<br><br>Prime factors:<br>2, 2, 2, 3, 3 | **a**   14<br><br><br><br>14 = _____<br><br>Prime factors:<br>_____ | **b**   6<br><br><br><br>6 = _____<br><br>Prime factors:<br>_____ | **c**   12<br><br><br><br>12 = _____<br><br>Prime factors:<br>_____ |
| **d**   20

20 = _____

Prime factors:
_____ | **e**   21

21 = _____

Prime factors:
_____ | **f**   81

81 = _____

Prime factors:
_____ | **g**   49

49 = _____

Prime factors:
_____ |
| **h**   80

80 = _____

Prime factors:
_____ | **i**   63

63 = _____

Prime factors:
_____ | **j**   45

45 = _____

Prime factors:
_____ | **k**   36

36 = _____

Prime factors:
_____ |

Lesson 25: Prime Factorization
```

Factors and Product Game

- <u>Player A:</u> Select a number from the box, draw an X over it, and write it under **Selected Number** as the selected product.
- Write as many factor pairs of the product as possible under **Multiplication Number Sentence** and list all of the factors under **List of the Factors.**
- Add the factors and write the sum under **Player A's Points.**
- <u>Player B:</u> Repeat steps 1–3.
- Alternate turns and continue to play until 18 of the numbers are crossed out. (A player can use a number crossed out by the other player ONLY if all of its factor pairs were not listed.)
- Add up all your points. The player with the most points is the winner.

Player A _____   **Player B** _____

2	3	4	5	6	7	8	9	10	11
12	13	14	15	16	17	18	19	20	21
22	23	25	26	27	29	30	31	35	37

Selected Number	Multiplication Number Sentence	List of the Factors	Player A's Points	Player B's Points
25	$1 \times 25, 5 \times 5$	1, 5, 25	31	

Total Points _____ _____

Lesson 25: Prime Factorization **121**

Prime Factor Game

- Player A: Select a number from the box, draw an X over it, and write it under **Selected Number** as the selected product. Draw a factor tree on scrap paper to find the prime factors of the product.
- Write the number's prime factorization under **Prime Factorization.**
- Count how many prime factors the product has and write that number as your points.
- Player B: Repeat steps 1–3.
- Alternate turns and continue to play until 18 of the numbers are crossed out.
- Add up all your points. The player with the most points is the winner.

Player A _____   Player B _____

4	6	8	9	10	12	14	15	16	18
20	21	24	25	26	27	28	30	32	35
36	40	42	45	48	49	54	56	64	~~81~~

Selected Number	Prime Factorization	Player A's Points	Player B's Points
81	3 × 3 × 3 × 3	4	
	Total Points:		

Lesson 25: Prime Factorization

Name_____   Date_____

Problem Solving & Practice: Factors

Solve each problem. Show your work. Draw a picture when needed.

a The prime factors of a number are 2, 2, 2, and 5. What is the number?

c Draw a factor tree for the number. Write a number sentence and list the prime factors of the number.

54 = _____

Prime factors: _____

b The prime factors of a number are 3, 3, 3, and 3. What is the number?

Draw a factor tree for each number.

d 28   **e** 100   **f** 42

Lesson 25: Prime Factorization 123

Name_____ Date_____

Lesson 25 Quiz

Draw a factor tree for the number and write the prime factorization of it.

Example:	**a** 15	**b** 18	**c** 25
| ```
       20
      /  \
    10    2
   /|     |
  5 2     2
```  20 = 5 × 2 × 2 | 15 = _____ | 18 = _____ | 25 = _____ |
d 64	**e** 16	**f** 26	**g** 30
64 = _____	16 = _____	26 = _____	30 = _____
h 32	**i** 35	**j** 40	**k** Create your own factor tree.
32 = _____	35 = _____	40 = _____	

124   Lesson 25: Prime Factorization
```

LESSON 26

Divide with Decimals

OBJECTIVES

Students will be introduced to division with decimals.

Students will practice dividing with decimals as the dividend and decimals as the divisor. Students will master how to divide when the dividend or the divisor is a decimal.

DIRECT INSTRUCTION

Give a set of **paper or plastic dollars, dimes, and pennies** to each small group. Have four students share $12.48 and discover that each student will get $3.12. Have them repeat this for $6.24 ÷ 2 and $10.30 ÷ 2. Write on the board $29\overline{)93.09}$, point out the decimal point in the dividend, and show students how to solve the problem. Tell them the first step is to estimate the quotient (90 ÷ 30 = 3), multiply it by the divisor, and subtract the product. Explain that the remaining 6 dollars must be changed into dimes to be divided by 29. Bring down the 0 in the dime's place, and write the decimal point after the 3 in the quotient. Estimate the quotient, and write 2 in the dime's place. Multiply 2 by the divisor and subtract. Explain that the remaining 29 is in the penny's place, so when it is divided by the divisor 29, you will write 1 in the penny's place. Repeat this with $38.40 ÷ 12 and $124.80 ÷ 39. Discuss the importance of the decimal point with the class.

Step 1	Step 2	Step 3
3	3.2	3.21
29)93.09	29)93.09	29)93.09
87	87	87
6	60	60
	58	58
	2	29

Show students how to divide when the divisor is a decimal. Write on the board $0.25\overline{)1.50}$, $25\overline{)150}$, and *One piece of gum costs a quarter. How many pieces can you buy with $1.50?* Explain that the two division problems are exactly the same, but one is written in dollars and the other in cents ($0.25 is 25 cents). Tell students that they can move the decimal point to the right in the divisor and the same number of places in the dividend to make decimals into whole numbers to simplify a division problem. Solve the problem on the board, and have the class solve 12.46 ÷ 0.2, 12.48 ÷ 0.04, and 12 ÷ 0.12.

GUIDED PRACTICE

✓ Have students work in small groups as you help them complete the **Dividing Dollars, Dimes, and Pennies reproducible (page 126).**

✓ Work with students in small groups to help them complete the **Divisors as Decimals reproducible (page 127).**

INDEPENDENT PRACTICE

✓ Invite groups of three students to play the **Decimal 4-in-a-Row Game (page 128).** Two students will play while the third player checks their answers using a **calculator.** Tell students to use **scrap paper** to compute quotients.

✓ Give each student the **Problem Solving & Practice: Divide with Decimals reproducible (page 129)** to complete independently.

ASSESSMENT

✓ Have students complete the **Lesson 26 Quiz (page 130)** in 10 minutes. Challenge students to "beat their time" and complete the quiz in less time and then again in even less time to show that they have mastered this new concept.

Lesson 26: Divide with Decimals   **125**

Name_____ Date_____

Dividing Dollars, Dimes, and Pennies

Example:

| $27\overline{)97.20}$

 Think.
 90 ÷ 30 = 3 | 3
 $27\overline{)97.20}$
 81
 $\overline{162}$

 Multiply and subtract. Bring down the 2 in the dime's place so you have 162 dimes. | 3.60
 $27\overline{)97.20}$
 81
 $\overline{162}$
 162
 $\overline{0}$

 Write the decimal point in the quotient and divide 162 by 27. The quotient is 3.60. |

Solve each problem. Think of division of decimals as equally sharing dollars, dimes, and pennies.

a	b	c	d	e
$4\overline{)\$12.44}$	$3\overline{)\$9.09}$	$2\overline{)\$1.16}$	$5\overline{)\$2.15}$	$3\overline{)\$54.42}$

f	g	h	i	j
$5\overline{)\$42.50}$	$50\overline{)\$52.50}$	$7\overline{)\$64.40}$	$70\overline{)\$64.40}$	$3\overline{)\$25.20}$

k	l	m	n	o
$30\overline{)\$25.20}$	$32\overline{)\$67.20}$	$39\overline{)\$97.50}$	$20\overline{)\$80.60}$	$59\overline{)\$88.50}$

Lesson 26: Divide with Decimals

Name_____ Date_____

Divisors as Decimals

Solve each problem by changing the decimal divisor to a whole number divisor. (Move the decimal point to the right the same number of places in the divisor and the dividend.)

Example: $0.3 \overline{)1.59} \longrightarrow 3 \overline{)15.9}$ with work showing $\begin{array}{r} 5.3 \\ 15 \\ \hline 0\,9 \\ 9 \\ \hline 0 \end{array}$	**a** $0.20 \overline{)1.54}$	**b** $0.4 \overline{)1.54}$
c $1.2 \overline{)25.2}$	**d** $1.2 \overline{)2.76}$	**e** $0.5 \overline{)25.65}$
f $5.6 \overline{)23.52}$	**g** $0.59 \overline{)3.54}$	**h** $0.05 \overline{)25.65}$
i $0.32 \overline{)1.632}$	**j** $0.51 \overline{)1.581}$	**k** $1.24 \overline{)3.72}$

Lesson 26: Divide with Decimals 127

Decimal 4-in-a-Row Game

- Choose one player to be Player O, one player to be Player X, and one player to be the judge.
- Player O: Begin the game by choosing a problem and solving it. (Change decimal divisors to whole numbers.)
- Judge: Use a calculator to check the quotient. If the quotient is correct, have Player O write an O in the box of the solved problem.
- Player X: If Player O's answer is not correct, solve the problem. Write an X in the box if the quotient is correct.
- Take turns and continue playing until a player correctly solves four problems in a row across, down, or on a diagonal.

Player O _____ Player X _____ Judge _____

a $4\overline{)3.48}$	b $3\overline{)39.09}$	c $2\overline{)21.16}$	d $5\overline{)12.15}$
e $1.2\overline{)6.36}$	f $5.6\overline{)34.16}$	g $0.12\overline{)25.2}$	h $0.59\overline{)3.54}$
i $7\overline{)45.50}$	j $30\overline{)35.10}$	k $1.2\overline{)3.96}$	l $0.21\overline{)0.651}$
m $19\overline{)72.20}$	n $1.4\overline{)9.24}$	o $20\overline{)112.60}$	p $2.12\overline{)7.632}$
q $5\overline{)100.50}$	r $70\overline{)45.50}$	s $5.6\overline{)23.52}$	t $1.2\overline{)25.2}$

Lesson 26: Divide with Decimals

Name_____ Date_____

Problem Solving & Practice: Divide with Decimals

Solve each problem. Show your work. Draw a picture when needed.

a Joseph has to drive 500.80 miles to get to his grandma's house. If he drives 40 miles each hour, how long will the drive take?

b Which of the following is the same as 300 ÷ 0.23?

A. 3,000 ÷ 23
B. 30,000 ÷ 23
C. 300,000 ÷ 23
D. 30 x 2.3

c Find the missing digit in the divisor.

$$4.?\overline{)25.2}^{6}$$

d Find the missing digits in the division problem. (Hint: There is no remainder. Estimate the quotient.)

$$5.?\overline{)31.8}^{?}$$

e Find the missing divisor.

$$?\overline{)85.5}^{9.5}$$

f You have $8.00. You want to buy tapes that are on sale for $1.65. How many tapes can you buy?

Lesson 26: Divide with Decimals **129**

Name_____   Date_____

Lesson 26 Quiz

Solve each problem.

a 79)483.48

b 31)260.71

c 19)4.75

d 61)91.50

e 7.9)11.85

f 3.1)26.66

g 1.9)4.37

h 3.2)131.84

i 42)67.20

j 2.1)115.50

These are the number facts I missed on the quiz:

Lesson 26: Divide with Decimals

Teacher Record Sheet

	Pretest	Lesson 1	Lesson 2	Lesson 3	Lesson 4	Lesson 5	Lesson 6	Lesson 7	Lesson 8	Lesson 9	Lesson 10	Lesson 11	Lesson 12	Lesson 13	Lesson 14	Lesson 15	Lesson 16	Lesson 17	Lesson 18	Lesson 19	Lesson 20	Lesson 21	Lesson 22	Lesson 23	Lesson 24	Lesson 25	Lesson 26	Cumulative Test

Name_____ Date_____

Pretest

Lesson 12: Use mental math to solve each problem.

6 × 14 = ____   7 × 21 = ____

Lesson 13: Circle the answer.

Which is a prime factor of

12?   20?

1, 3, 7, 12   4, 5, 10, 20

Lesson 14

32 × 40 = ____   51 × 30 = ____

Lesson 15

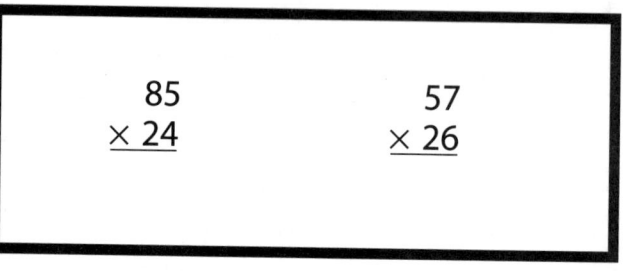

$$\begin{array}{r} 85 \\ \times\ 24 \end{array} \qquad \begin{array}{r} 57 \\ \times\ 26 \end{array}$$

Lesson 16: Estimate the product using compatible factors.

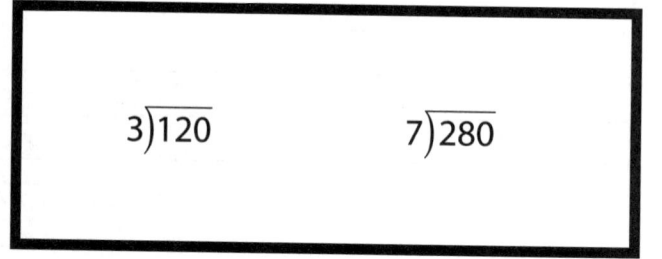

$$\begin{array}{r} 51 \\ \times\ 18 \end{array} \qquad \begin{array}{r} 58 \\ \times\ 38 \end{array}$$

Lesson 17

3)120   7)280

Lesson 18

60)240   70)350

Lesson 19

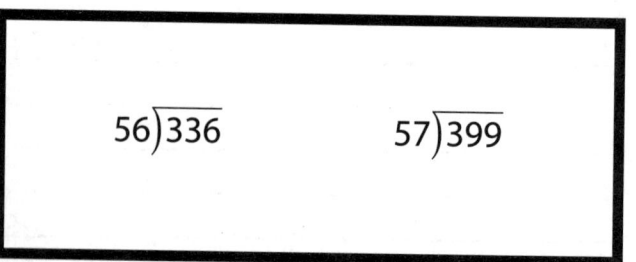

56)336   57)399

Lesson 20

$10^2 + 4^2$ = ____

$\sqrt{100} \div \sqrt{25}$ = ____

Lesson 21: List the multiples and find the least common multiple (LCM).

30:
40:                    LCM = ____

6:
4:                     LCM = ____

132   Assessment

Name_____ Date_____

Pretest

Lesson 22

```
  0.25        3.55
×    8      × 1.8
```

Lesson 23

Find the sales tax of a $200 purchase. The tax rate is 6%.

Find the sale price of a bike. Its price is $200. It is on sale for 30% off.

Lesson 24: Estimate the answers using compatible numbers for the percents.

99% of 300   19% of 400

Lesson 25: Draw a factor tree and write the prime factorization (e.g., $20 = 2 \times 2 \times 5$).

12   32

12 = _____   32 = _____

Lesson 26

$7 \overline{)64.40}$ $1.9 \overline{)4.37}$

Assessment 133

Name_____   Date_____

Cumulative Test

Solve each problem.

| **a)** $0 \times 5 =$ ___ | **b)** $1 \times 3 =$ ___ | **c)** $2 \times 10 =$ ___ | **d)** $7 \times 4 =$ ___ |
| **e)** $6 \times 8 =$ ___ | **f)** $42 \div 7 =$ ___ | **g)** $9 \div 1 =$ ___ | **h)** $24 \div 3 =$ ___ |

Draw a circle around each prime number. Draw a box around each composite number.

i) 2   4   5   6   9   11   15   19   21   22   29   34   45   67

Solve each problem.

| **j)** 24 $\times$ 20 | **k)** 16 $\times$ 30 | **l)** 32 $\times$ 21 | **m)** 72 $\times$ 32 | **n)** 0.25 $\times$ 13 |
| **o)** 30.15 $\times$ 5 | **p)** $2^2 + 3^2 =$ ___ | **q)** $\sqrt{25} - \sqrt{9} =$ ___ | **r)** $4^2 \div \sqrt{64} =$ ___ | **s)** $\sqrt{100} \times 5^2 =$ ___ |

t) Find the sales tax of a $12.60 purchase. The sales tax rate is 5%.

u) Find the sale price of a stereo. The sale price is 20% off the original price of $350.

v) A $145 coat is on sale for 30% off. The sales tax is 6%. How much will you pay?

Solve each problem. Use compatible divisors to estimate quotients when needed.

| **w)** $9\overline{)360}$ | **x)** $5\overline{)2500}$ | **y)** $4\overline{)2000}$ | **z)** $30\overline{)120}$ |
| **aa)** $80\overline{)560}$ | **bb)** $70\overline{)490}$ | **cc)** $48\overline{)144}$ | **dd)** $40\overline{)258}$ |

ee) Find the LCM.
4:
6:
LCM = ___

ff) Find the LCD and solve.
$\frac{1}{9} + \frac{1}{6} =$

gg) Draw a factor tree for each number.
30   100

134 Assessment

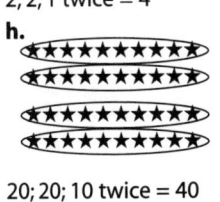

Answer Key

Page 9

f, a, d, g, c, e, b
h. 0 1 10 4
i. 0 2 20 0
j. 0 3 30 10
k. 0 4 40 5
l. 0 5 50 90
m. 0 6 60 6
n. 0 7 70 0
o. 0 8 80 20
p. 0 9 90 1
q. 0 10 100 0
r. The answer is 0.
s. The answer is the number being multiplied by 1.
t. Place a zero to the right of the number being multiplied by 10 to find the answer.

Page 10 Lesson 1 Quiz

a. 4   **b.** 0   **c.** 40   **d.** 0
e. 7   **f.** 90 **g.** 8   **h.** 30
i. 80 **j.** 60
e, c, f, b, a, d, g

Page 12

a. 2 x 5 = 10; 5 x 2 = 10
b. 5 x 2 = 10; 2 x 5 = 10
c. 2 x 6 = 12; 6 x 2 = 12
d. 2 x 6 = 12; 6 x 2 = 12
e.
(X X X X)
(X X X X)
f.
(X X) (X X) (X X) (X X)
(X X) (X X) (X X) (X X)
g. 2; 1 x 2 = 2   **h.** 0; 0 x 2 = 0
i. 14; 2 x 7 = 14   **j.** 20; 10 x 2 = 20
k. 18; 9 x 2 = 18   **l.** 4; 2 x 2 = 4
m. 6; 2 x 3 = 6   **n.** 16; 8 x 2 = 16
o. 12; 2 x 6 = 12   **p.** 8; 4 x 2 = 8
q. 10; 2 x 5 = 10   **r.** 0; 2 x 0 = 0

Page 13 Lesson 2 Quiz

a. 8   **b.** 2
c. 10 **d.** 12
e. 14 **f.** 18
g. 0   **h.** 6
i. 16 **j.** 20
k. 5   **l.** 0

m. 30 **n.** 0
o. 7   **p.** 0
q. 8   **r.** 4
s. 80 **t.** 60

Page 15

Value of nickels 5¢, 10¢, 15¢, 20¢, 25¢, 30¢, 35¢, 40¢, 45¢, 50¢
a. 1 x 5 = 5; 5 x 1 = 5
b. 2 x 5 = 10; 5 x 2 = 10
c. 3 x 5 = 15; 5 x 3 = 15
d. 4 x 5 = 20; 5 x 4 = 20
e. 5 x 5 = 25; 5 x 5 = 25
f. 6 x 5 = 30; 5 x 6 = 30
g. 7 x 5 = 35; 5 x 7 = 35
h. 8 x 5 = 40; 5 x 8 = 40
i. 9 x 5 = 45; 5 x 9 = 45
j. 10 x 5 = 50; 5 x 10 = 50
How many minutes? 5, 15, 30, 45, 20, 25, 35, 40, 50, 55, 60

Page 16 Lesson 3 Quiz

a. 10 **b.** 5
c. 15 **d.** 20
e. 35 **f.** 45
g. 40 **h.** 30
i. 25 **j.** 50

k. 4   **l.** 16
m. 10 **n.** 8
o. 10 **p.** 18
q. 14 **r.** 0
s. 0   **t.** 0

Page 18

a. 9   **b.** 90 **c.** 81
d. 45 **e.** 72 **f.** 18
g. 27 **h.** 54 **i.** 63
j. 0   **k.** 36 **l.** 45
m. 27 **n.** 9   **o.** 63
p. 45 **q.** 18 **r.** 90
s. 54 **t.** 0   **u.** 36

Page 19 Lesson 4 Quiz

a. 18 **b.** 63
c. 72 **d.** 54
e. 9   **f.** 45
g. 36 **h.** 27
i. 90 **j.** 0
k. 10 **l.** 25
m. 30 **n.** 81
o. 14 **p.** 7
q. 0   **r.** 6
s. 9   **t.** 80

Page 21

b.
16; 16; 8 twice = 32
c.
14; 14; 7 twice = 28
d.
12; 12; 6 twice = 24
e.
8; 8; 4 twice = 16
f.
6; 6; 3 twice = 12
g.
2; 2; 1 twice = 4
h.
20; 20; 10 twice = 40

Page 22 Lesson 5 Quiz

a. 4   **b.** 20
c. 28 **d.** 24
e. 40 **f.** 32
g. 0   **h.** 12
i. 16 **j.** 36
k. 10 **l.** 36
m. 30 **n.** 5
o. 8   **p.** 6
q. 0   **r.** 63
s. 20 **t.** 18

Page 24

a.

6, 9

b.

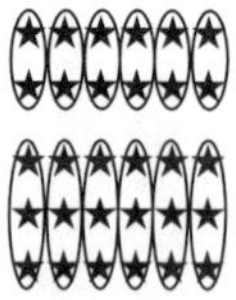

12, 18

c.

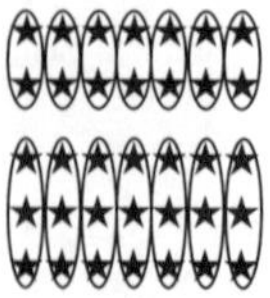

14, 21

d.

16, 24

a. 93 **b.** 24 **c.** 210 **d.** 66 **e.** 33
f. 126 **g.** 159 **h.** 189 **i.** 48 **j.** 75

Page 25 Lesson 6 Quiz

a. 6 **b.** 3
c. 27 **d.** 12
e. 21 **f.** 15
g. 24 **h.** 18
i. 9 **j.** 30
k. 0 **l.** 6
m. 18 **n.** 7
o. 40 **p.** 20
q. 1 **r.** 81
s. 25 **t.** 80

Page 27

a. 30; 36
b. 20; 24
c. 40; 48
d. 10; 12
e. 36 **f.** 66 **g.** 540 **h.** 300
i. 192 **j.** 510 **k.** 162 **l.** 96

Page 28 Lesson 7 Quiz

a. 12 **b.** 42
c. 18 **d.** 6
e. 30 **f.** 60
g. 54 **h.** 36
i. 0 **j.** 24
k. 24 **l.** 12
m. 0 **n.** 6
o. 48 **p.** 15
q. 81 **r.** 5
s. 20 **t.** 14

Page 30

b, g, e, c, f, a, d
a. 56 **b.** 560 **c.** 427 **d.** 416
e. 768 **f.** 119 **g.** 664 **h.** 175

Page 31 Lesson 8 Quiz

a. 16 **b.** 64
c. 63 **d.** 49
e. 42 **f.** 56
g. 24 **h.** 21
i. 8 **j.** 28
k. 3 **l.** 40
m. 36 **n.** 32
o. 35 **p.** 72
q. 12 **r.** 0
s. 8 **t.** 36

Page 33

b.

18 ÷ 3 = 6; Each person gets 6¢.

c.

24 ÷ 2 = 12; Each person gets 12¢.

d.

21 ÷ 3 = 7; Each person gets 7¢.

e.

16 ÷ 2 = 8; Each person gets 8¢.

f.

15 ÷ 3 = 5; Each person gets 5¢.
g. 20 ÷ 2 = 10; Each person gets 10¢;
2 people x 10¢ = 20¢.
h. 27 ÷ 3 = 9; Each person gets 9¢;
3 people x 9¢ = 27¢.
i. 22 ÷ 2 = 11; Each person gets 11¢;
2 people x 11¢ = 22¢.

Page 34 Lesson 9 Quiz

a. 5 **b.** 4
c. 6 **d.** 4
e. 6 **f.** 9
g. 9 **h.** 8
i. 7 **j.** 3
k. 16 **l.** 24
m. 14 **n.** 21
o. 36 **p.** 64
q. 40 **r.** 28
s. 27 **t.** 12

Page 36

a.

20 ÷ 4 = 5; 5 teams; 4 x 5 = 20

b.

15 ÷ 5 = 3; 3 cages; 3 x 5 = 15

c.

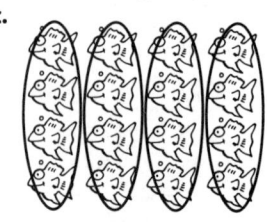

16 ÷ 4 = 4; 4 bowls; 4 x 4 = 16

d.

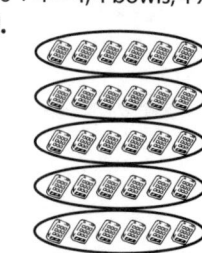

30 ÷ 6 = 5; 5 boxes; 6 x 5 = 30

e.

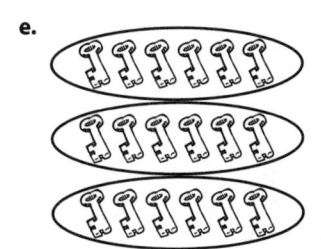

18 ÷ 6 = 3; 3 key rings; 3 x 6 = 18

f.

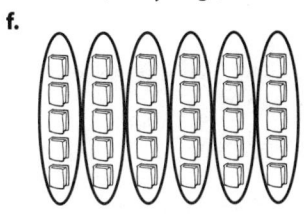

30 ÷ 5 = 6; 6 shelves; 6 x 5 = 30
g. $32.00 ÷ $4.00 = 8; 8 days; 8 x $4.00 = $32.00
h. $42.00 ÷ 6 = $7.00; Each person gets $7.00; 6 x $7.00 = $42.00
i. 40 ÷ 5 = 8; 8 days; 8 x 5 = 40

Page 37 Lesson 10 Quiz
a. 2 **b.** 7
c. 4 **d.** 8
e. 3 **f.** 6
g. 5 **h.** 9
i. 8 **j.** 7
k. 40 **l.** 40
m. 21 **n.** 0
o. 64 **p.** 18
q. 72 **r.** 7
s. 54 **t.** 16

Page 39
a.

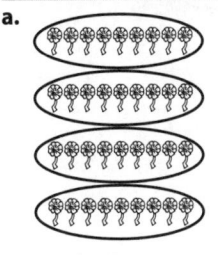

36 ÷ 9 = 4; 4 vases; 4 x 9 = 36
b.

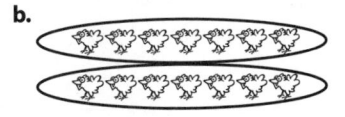

14 ÷ 7 = 2; 2 tree branches; 2 x 7 = 14
c.

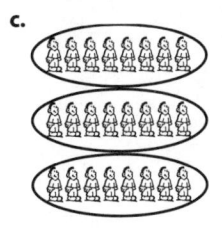

24 ÷ 8 = 3; 3 rafts; 3 x 8 = 24
d.

16 ÷ 8 = 2; 2 bowls of food; 2 x 8 = 16
e. 42 ÷ 7 = 6; $6; $6 x 7 people = $42
f. 64 ÷ 8 = 8; 8 days; 8 days x $8 = 64
g. 72 ÷ 9 = 8; 8 cards; 8 cards x 9 envelopes = 72 cards

Page 40 Lesson 11 Quiz
a. 1 **b.** 8
c. 7 **d.** 5
e. 6 **f.** 9
g. 10 **h.** 2
i. 6 **j.** 10
k. 9 **l.** 2
m. 3 **n.** 8
o. 6 **p.** 8
q. 9 **r.** 5
s. 7 **t.** 4

Page 42
a. 20; 40; 30; 50; 42
b. 30; 60; 72; 39; 45
c. 40; 80; 48; 92; 104
d. 50; 100; 75; 55; 135
e. 60; 120; 144; 102; 132
f. 70; 140; 175; 161; 91
g. 80; 160; 168; 96; 144
h. 90; 180; 144; 207; 108
i. 100; 150; 225; 36; 800

Page 43
42	56	108
50	88	198
68	164	180
84	44	287
106	280	350
114	128	91
120	216	189
76	210	126
48	155	160
28	125	112
26	115	256
66	75	136
39	230	328
90	100	117
33	96	225
93	132	378
30	66	171
48	156	324

Page 45
a. 3, 2, 6, 9, 18
b. 2, 4, **6**, 8, 10; 3, **6**, 9, 12, 15
c. 6 bags **d.** 84
e. 126 **f.** 51 **g.** 110
h. 64 **i.** 231 **j.** 200
k. 126 **l.** 184 **m.** 108
n. 66 **o.** 20 **p.** 48
q. 123 **r.** 420 **s.** 32

Page 46 Lesson 12 Quiz
a. 84 **b.** 147
c. 488 **d.** 369
e. 210 **f.** 357
g. 16, 24, 32, 40, 48
h. 12, 18, 24, 30, 36
i. 10, 15, 20, 25, 30
j. 20, 30, 40, 50, 60

Page 48
2, 3, 5, 7, 11, 13, 17, 19, 23, 29, 31, 37, 41, 43, 47, 53, 59, 61, 67, 71, 73, 79, 83, 89, 97

Page 49
6; composite; 2 x 3 = 6
7; prime; 7 x 1 = 7; no other factors
9; prime; 9 x 1 = 9; no other factors
11; prime; 11 x 1 = 11; no other factors
12; composite; 6 x 2 = 12; 4 x 3 = 12
13; prime; 13 x 1 = 13 no other factors
15; composite; 5 x 3 = 15
16; composite; 8 x 2 = 16; 4 x 4 = 16
17; prime; 17 x 1 = 17; no other factors
a. 2 **b.** 5 **c.** 5
d. 3 **e.** 7 **f.** 7
g. 14 **h.** 200 **i.** 40

Page 51
a. 3 **b.** 12
c. 6 **d.** 29
composite: 8, 15, 10, 21, 25, 9
prime: 5, 19, 29, 7

Page 52 Lesson 13 Quiz
prime: 3, 5, 7, 11, 13, 17, 19, 23
a. 3 **b.** 5 **c.** 5
d. 3 **e.** 7 **f.** 7

Page 54
a. 63; 630
b. 48; 480
c. 82; 820
d. 42; 420
e. 270; 2,700
f. 180; 1,800
g. 153; 1,530
h. 119; 1,190

i. 352; 3,520

a. 420 b. 810 c. 2,080
d. 620 e. 1,080 f. 520
g. 2,200 h. 1,560 i. 480
j. 800

Page 55
a. 1,820 b. 540 c. 1,420
d. 1,620 e. 1,280 f. 930
g. 1,830 h. 870 i. 1,950
j. 2,340 k. 1,240 l. 680
m. 2,880 n. 1,320 o. 600
p. 2,150 q. 4,350 r. 4,500
s. 1,600 t. 4,250

a. 426; 4,260 b. 842; 8,420
c. 786; 7,860 d. 987; 9,870
e. 3,200; 32,000
f. 2,964; 29,640
g. 1,863; 18,630
h. 3,507; 35,070

Page 57
a. 25 x 30 = 750 water balloons
b. 19 x 50 = 950 gallons of gas
c. 12 x 30 = 360 cards
d. 90 x 56 = 5,040 pieces of popcorn
e. 2,480 f. 6,390 g. 5,280
h. 3,150 i. 2,640 j. 1,020
k. 660 l. 1,650

Page 58 Lesson 14 Quiz
a. 1,280 b. 1,530 c. 4,960
d. 2,940 e. 2,250 f. 4,270
g. 420 h. 5,920 i. 1,440
j. 530
k. 7 l. 5 m. 5
n. 2 o. 5 p. 5
q. 16 r. 20 s. 40

Page 60
a. 32; 640; 672
b. 68; 1,020; 1088
c. 126; 840; 966
d. 159; 1,590; 1,749
e. 52; 2,080; 2,132
f. 48; 120; 168
g. 144; 1,440; 1,584
h. 224; 1,280; 1504

Page 61
a. 792 b. 672
c. 588 d. 1,800
e. 3,162 f. 882
g. 2,015 h. 3,060
i. 2,116 j. 1,170

k. 2,090 l. 1,806
m. 1,134 n. 444
o. 2,394 p. 3,276
q. 924 r. 1,440
s. 2,108 t. 1,890

Page 63
a. 25 x 35 = 875 pieces of trash
b. 19 x 45 = 855 peanuts
c. 12 x 37 = 444 dolls
d. 660; 720
Multiply the smaller number by 30.
e. 1,606 f. 1,472 g. 1,320
h. 2,522 i. 814 j. 2,772
k. 2,322 l. 3,825

Page 64 Lesson 15 Quiz
a. 1,166 b. 3,888 c. 2,106
d. 1,196 e. 1,508 f. 1,075
g. 2,660 h. 1,890
i. 4,512 j. 3,933

Page 66
a. 40 x 20 = 800
b. 50 x 20 = 1,000
c. 60 x 20 = 1,200
d. 40 x 10 = 400
e. 60 x 20 = 1,200
f. 770 x 20 = 15,400
g. 450 x 80 = 36,000
h. 600 x 50 = 30,000
i. 400 x 30 = 12,000
j. 350 x 30 = 10,500
k. 500 x 30 = 15,000

a. 50 x 5 = $250
b. 40 x 5 = $200
c. 20 x 9 = $180
d. 30 x 6 = $180
e. 40 x 8 = $320

Page 67
a. 30 x 20 = 600
b. 20 x 20 = 400
c. 20 x 40 = 800
d. 50 x 30 = 1,500
e. 60 x 30 = 1,800
f. 10 x 60 = 600
g. 20 x 60 = 1,200
h. 70 x 40 = 2,800
i. 20 x 90 = 1,800
j. 30 x 70 = 2,100
k. 40 x 70 = 2,800
l. 30 x 10 = 300
m. 40 x 50 = 2,000
n. 60 x 30 = 1,800
o. 80 x 20 = 1,600

Page 69
a. 30 x 30 = 900 books
b. 50 x 20 = 1,000 sprinkles
c. 90 x 2 = $180.00
d. 80 x 2 = $160.00
e. 40 x 3 = 120
f. 40 x 8 = 320
g. 300 x 6 = 1,800
h. 400 x 3 = 1,200
i. 500 x 2 = 1,000

Page 70 Lesson 16 Quiz
a. 50 x 20 = 1,000
b. 60 x 40 = 2,400
c. 800 x 20 = 16,000
d. 500 x 20 = 10,000
e. 100 x 60 = 6,000

a. 20 x 3 = 60
b. 60 x 3 = 180
c. 30 x 2 = 60
d. 40 x 8 = 320
e. 80 x 4 = 320

Page 72
a. 2; 2 tens; 2 hundreds
2; 20; 200
b. 2; 2 tens; 2 hundreds
2; 20; 200
c. 5; 5 tens; 5 hundreds
5; 50; 500
d. 2; 2 tens; 2 hundreds
2; 20; 200
e. 4; 4 tens; 4 hundreds
4; 40; 400

Page 73
a. 5; 50; 500
b. 7; 70; 700
c. 3; 30; 300
d. 7; 70; 700
e. 4; 40; 400
f. 20; 200; 2,000
g. 10; 100; 1,000
h. 7; 70; 700
i. 6; 60; 600
j. 8; 80; 800
k. 9; 90; 900
l. 9; 90; 900
m. 10; 100; 1,000; 10,000
n. 4; 40; 400; 4,000
o. 2; 20; 200; 2,000

Page 75
a. $4,000
b. $6 million
c. 100 trays
d. 3,000 students

e. 50 f. 10 g. 80 h. 80 i. 70
j. 30 k. 30 l. 50 m. 30 n. 40

Page 76 Lesson 17 Quiz
a. 40   b. 50
c. 40   d. 40
e. 90   f. 200
g. 100 h. 40
i. 50   j. 50

Page 78
a. 4; 4
b. 20; 20
c. 10; 10
d. 70; 70
e. 50; 50
f. 30; 30
g. 2; 2
h. 30; 30
i. 40; 40
j. 8; 8
k. 40; 40
l. 8; 8

Page 79
a. 1; 1; 1; 1
b. 4; 4; 4; 4
c. 8; 8; 8; 8
d. 3; 3; 3; 3
e. 4; 4; 4; 4
f. 9; 9; 9; 9
g. 5; 5; 5; 5
h. 5; 5; 5; 5
i. 8; 8; 8; 8

Page 81
a. 6 friends   b. 90
c. 40 friends d. D.

e. 7 f. 6 g. 8 h. 5 i. 30
j. 9 k. 3 l. 6 m. 6 n. 4

Page 82 Lesson 18 Quiz
a. 7   b. 5
c. 6   d. 4
e. 5   f. 2
g. 9   h. 21
i. 14 j. 7
k. 20 l. 60
m. 40 n. 100
o. 60

Page 84
a. 113 ÷ 50;
11 ÷ 5 = 2;
113 ÷ 48 = 2 R17
b. 426 ÷ 60;
42 ÷ 6 = 7;
426 ÷ 58 = 7 R20
c. 401 ÷ 80;
40 ÷ 8 = 5;
401 ÷ 79 = 5 R6
d. 241 ÷ 60;
24 ÷ 6 = 4;
241 ÷ 59 = 4 R5
e. 89 ÷ 40;
8 ÷ 4 = 2;
89 ÷ 42 = 2 R5

Page 85
a. 240 ÷ 50;
24 ÷ 5 = 4;
240 ÷ 46 = 5;
240 ÷ 46 = 5 R10
b. 296 ÷ 30;
29 ÷ 3 = 9;
296 ÷ 33 = 8;
296 ÷ 33 = 8 R32
c. 168 ÷ 30;
16 ÷ 3 = 5;
168 ÷ 27 = 6;
168 ÷ 27 = 6 R6
d. 310 ÷ 60;
31 ÷ 6 = 5;
310 ÷ 63 = 4;
310 ÷ 63 = 4 R58
e. 153 ÷ 20;
15 ÷ 2 = 7;
153 ÷ 24 = 6;
153 ÷ 24 = 6 R9

Page 86
a. 6, 2, 4, 7
b. 8, 3, 5, 7
c. 3, 6, 6, 5
d. 5, 3, 5, 6
e. 4, 2, 8, 7

Page 87
a. C.   b. C.
c. 378 ÷ 42 = 9
d. 306 ÷ 51 = 6
e. 372 ÷ 93 = 4
f. 1581 ÷ 51 = 31

Page 88 Lesson 19 Quiz
a. 3   b. 8
c. 9   d. 3
e. 7   f. 2
g. 10 h. 4
i. 11 j. 8

Page 90

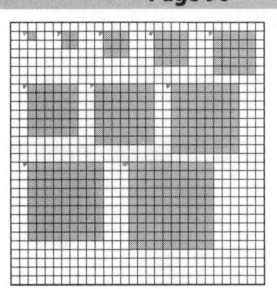

Page 91
a. 4 x 4 = 16; 4
b. 0 x 0 = 0; 0
c. 10 x 10 = 100; 10
d. 3 x 3 = 9; 3
e. 9 x 9 = 81; 9
f. 8 x 8 = 64; 8
g. 7 x 7 = 49; 7
h. 6 x 6 = 36; 6
i. 12 x 12 = 144; 12
j. (5 x 5) + 5 = 30
k. (0 x 0) x 5 = 0
l. 10 x (4 x 4) = 160
m. 6 x (2 x 2) = 24
n. 9 + (5 x 5) = 34
o. (5 x 5) - 5 = 20
p. 7 x 5 = 35
q. 10 + (5 x 5) = 35
r. (5 x 5) x 2 = 50

Page 92
a. 100 b. 20
c. 8   d. 16
e. 18   f. 25
g. 10   h. 36
i. 50   j. 0
k. 60   l. 50
m. 18   n. 4
o. 90   p. 6
q. 50   r. 9
s. 38   t. 12
u. 0   v. 8
w. 5   x. 3
y. 18   z. 12
aa. 20 bb. 6
cc. 120 dd. 18
ee. 144 ff. 5
gg. 25 hh. 25

Answer Key   139

Page 93
a. 2 x 8 = 16; 4^2 pencils
b. 1st squirrel = 8; 2nd squirrel = 4; 8 + 4 = 12; 12 acorns
c. 6^2 = 36 shells
d. (5 x 7) – 5 = 30
e. 6   f. 2
g. 8   h. 16
i. 49   j. 81
k. 34   l. 64
m. 12   n. 5

Page 94 Lesson 20 Quiz
a. 116   b. 2
c. 40   d. 32
e. 13   f. 125
g. 12   h. 15
i. 125   j. 30
k. 28   l. 2
m. 144   n. 27
o. 225   p. 16

Page 96
a. 5, 10; 10; LCM = 10
b. 2: 2, 4, 6, 8, 10
10: 10
LCM = 10
c. 4: 4, 8, 12
6: 6, 12
LCM = 12
d. 2: 2, 4, 6
6: 6
LCM = 6
e. 5: 5, 10, 15, 20, 25, 30
6: 6, 12, 18, 24, 30
LCM = 30
f. 15: 15, 30
10: 10, 20, 30
LCM = 30
g. 3: 3, 6
6: 6
LCM = 6
h. 3: 3, 6, 9
9: 9
LCM = 9
i. 3: 3, 6, 9, 12
12: 12
LCM = 12
j. 4: 4, 8, 12, 16, 20
10: 10, 20
LCM = 20
k. 4: 4, 8, 12, 16, 20
5: 5, 10, 15, 20
LCM = 20
l. 5: 5, 10, 15
15: 15
LCM = 15

m. 18: 18
6: 6, 12, 18
LCM = 18
n. 7: 7, 14, 21
21: 21
LCM = 21
o. 8: 8, 16, 24
12: 12, 24
LCM = 24
p. 4: 4, 8, 12, 16, 20, 24
8: 8, 16, 24
12: 12, 24
LCM = 24
q. 4: 4, 8, 12, 16, 20, 24
12: 12, 24
24: 24
LCM = 24

Page 97
a. 1/5 = 2/10; 2/10 - 1/10 = 1/10
b. 1/2 = 4/8; 1/8 + 4/8 = 5/8
c. 1/2 = 5/10; 5/10 – 1/10 = 4/10
d. 1/6 = 2/12; 2/12 – 1/12 = 1/12
e. 1/10 = 2/20; 1/20 + 2/10 = 3/20
f. 1/15 = 2/30; 2/30 + 1/30 = 3/30 or 1/10
g. 1/50 = 2/100; 2/100 - 1/100 = 1/100
h. 1/6 = 3/18; 3/18 – 1/18 = 2/18 or 1/9
i. 1/10 = 3/30; 1/30 + 3/30 = 4/30 or 2/15
j. 1/5 = 5/25; 1/5 + 5/25 = 6/25
k. 3/5 = 6/10; 6/10 - 3/10 = 3/10
l. 1/12 = 3/36; 1/18 = 2/36; 3/36 – 2/36 = 1/36
m. 1/9 = 3/27; 3/27 + 1/27 = 4/27
n. 1/5 = 3/15; 1/15 + 3/15 = 4/15
o. 7/25 = 14/50; 1/10 = 5/50; 14/50 – 5/50 = 9/50
p. 1/5 = 20/100; 20/100 - 1/100 = 19/100
q. 1/10 = 10/100; 1/100 + 10/100 = 11/100

Page 98
a. 11/60
b. 1/16
c. 5/16
d. 1/24
e. 5/30
f. 1/18
g. 1/24
h. 7/24
i. 10/60 or 1/6
j. 3/12 or 1/4

Page 99
a. movie #1: 12:00; 2:00; 4:00; **6:00**; 8:00
movie #2: 12:00; 3:00; **6:00**
b. Track A: 4 minutes; 8 minutes; **12** minutes
Track B: 6 minutes; **12** minutes
c. Aussie: 3, 6, 9, 12; Aussie: 4 bones
4: Magic: 4, 8, 12; Magic: 3 bones
d. Lucy drove 2 hours @ 30 mph. She drove 60 miles.
At 20 mph, Betty will need 3 hours to drive 60 miles. She will arrive at 8:00 p.m.
e. 2: 2, 4, 6
3: 3, 6
LCM = 6
f. 4: 4, 8, 12, 16, 20, 24, 28
7: 7, 14, 21, 28
LCM = 28
g. 3: 3, 6, 9, 12, 15
5: 5, 10, 15
LCM = 15
h. 2: 2, 4, 6, 8, 10, 12, 14, 16, 18
9: 9, 18
LCM = 18

Page 100 Lesson 21 Quiz
a. 3: 3, 6, 9, 12, 15
5: 5, 10, 15
LCM = 15
b. 4: 4, 8, 12
6: 6, 12
LCM = 12
c. 8: 8, 16, 24
12: 12, 24
LCM = 24
d. 3: 3, 6, 9, 12, 15, 18, 21, 24, 27, 30
10: 10, 20, 30
LCM = 30
e. 45: 45, 90
90: 90
LCM = 90

f. 5/24   g. 3/40   h. 23/24
i. 13/60   j. 11/12

Page 102
a. 50¢; $0.50
b. 75¢; $.75
c. 100¢; $1.00
d. 125¢; $1.25
e. 150¢; $1.50
f. 175¢; $1.75
g. 200¢; $2.00
h. 225¢; $2.25
i. 250¢; $2.50
j. 275¢; $2.75

k. 300¢; $3.00
l. 325¢; $3.25
m. $2.50
n. $6.75
o. $16.25
p. $4.84
q. $6.25
r. $2.10
s. $6.60
t. $31.25
u. $28.84
v. $46.25
w. $20.50
x. $60.75
y. $151.25
z. $40.84
aa. $501.25

Page 103
a. 9.75; 0.650; 10.400
b. 4.42; 1.105; 5.525
c. 21.00; 0.840; 21.840
d. 9.00; .750; 9.750
e. 35.00; 2.500; 37.500
f. 12.8; 0.960; 13.760
g. 71.00; 5.680; 76.680
h. 3.00; 0.050; 3.050

Page 104
a. 1.00 b. 0.0050 c. 0.0250
d. 0.72 e. 0.0123 f. 89.20
g. 12.48 h. 0.864 i. 0.892
j. 37.87 k. 1.560 l. 0.2175
m. 12.75 n. 0.1072 o. 26.25
p. 37.50 q. 0.2889 r. 1.624
s. 22.88 t. 0.4060 u. 28.98
v. 8.24 w. 0.1236 x. 14.25
y. 44.05 z. .0525 aa. 34.08

Page 105
a. 3 adults x $5.60 = $16.80
2 children x $2.80 = $5.60
$16.80 + $5.60 = $22.40
b. 7 days x .45 inches = 3.15 inches
c. 64.5 miles x 8.5 hours = 548.25 miles
d. 10 bags x $1.75 = $17.50
e. 200 posters x $1.90 = $380.00
f. .28, .30
Number "a" is divided by 10 to get number "b."

Page 106 Lesson 22 Quiz
a. 1.00 b. 2.00 c. 2.65
d. 3.69 e. 9.88 f. 0.27
g. 0.92 h. 1.02 i. 0.75
j. 4.15 k. 21.30 l. 514.00
m. 250.00 n. 186.30 o. 434.00

Page 108
a. $2.50 b. $10.00 c. $20.00
d. $50.00 e. $0.24 f. $3.00
g. $30.00 h. $2.05 i. $250.00
j. $24.00 k. $1.50 l. $0.53
m. $3.20 n. $2.40 o. $450.00
p. $2.03 q. $1.52
r. $3.03 s. $12.00 t. $24.03
u. $60.00 v. $0.29 w. $3.60
x. $36.00 y. $2.45 z. $300.00
aa. $28.80 bb. $1.80

Page 109
a. $18.90
b. $320.00
c. $1.50
d. $49.50
e. $240.00
f. $360.30
g. $59.40
h. $16.00
i. $24.30
j. $180.00
k. $48.00
l. $6.30
m. $54.00
n. $16.40
o. $120.30
p. $36.00

Page 110
a. 0.50 b. .06 = 12.00 c. .07 = 2.835
d. 5.00 e. .06 = 24.00 f. .07 = 0.74
g. 10.00 h. .06 = 18.00 i. .07 = 0.62
j. 15.00 k. .06 = 1.20 l. .07 = 0.31
m. 21.00 n. .06 = 3.60 o. .07 = 0.57
p. 3.00 q. .06 = 1.23 r. .07 = 1.47
s. 2.00 t. .06 = 12.03 u. .07 = 3.85

Page 111
a. $12.00 x .05 = .60; $12.00 + .60 = $12.60
b. $15.00 x .06 = .90; $15.90 - $15.50 = .40; No, you are 40¢ short.
c. $150 x .40 = $60; $150 - $60 = $90.00
d. $120.99 x .06 = 7.26; choice C.
e. $100 x .40 = $40; $100 - $40 = $60; $60 x .07 = $4.20; $60 + 4.20 = $64.20
f. $20 x .20 = $4.00; $20 - $4 = $16; $16.00 x .06 = .96; $16.00 + .96 = $16.96

Page 112 Lesson 23 Quiz
a. $18.00 b. $1.09
c. $80.00 d. $320.00
e. $90.00 f. $140.00

Page 114
a. 99 x .25 = 24.75
b. 70 x .30 = 21.00
c. 70 x .20 = 14.00
d. 70 x .20 = 14.00
e. 72 x .25 = 18.00
f. 100 x .20 = 20.00
g. 99 x .20 = 19.80
h. 100 x .20 = 20.00
i. 200 x .20 = 40.00
j. 10 x .90 = 90.90
k. 100 x .80 = 80.00
l. 307 x .10 = 30.70
m. 810 x .10 = 81.00
n. 210 x .45 = 94.50
o. 300 x .90 = 270.00
p. 400 x .90 = 360.00
q. 607 x .10 = 60.70
r. 610 x .50 = 305.00
s. 510 x .50 = 255.00
t. 85 x .10 = 8.50
u. 97 x .50 = 48.50
v. 40 x .20 = 8.00
w. 89 x .20 = 17.80
x. 685 x .20 = 137.00

Page 115
a. 10.30 k. 10.00
b. 6.00 l. 75.25
c. 6.60 m. 60.15
d. 252 n. 2.10
e. 302 o. 60.10
f. 120.60 p. 17.50
g. 317.60 q. 195.50
h. 70.30 r. 90.50
i. 91.50 s. 122.75
j. 81.10 t. 152

Page 116
4	9.9	19.80	81
9.3	23.75	155	303
141.4	80	9.4	7.2
201	2.4	6.8	62.40
31.25	100.25	40.6	25.5

Page 117
a. 2,600,000
b. 1,700,000
c. 1,900,000
d. 6,800,000
e. 7,200,000
f. 400,000
g. 3,400,000
h. 3,600,000
i. 200,000

Page 118 Lesson 24 Quiz
a. 270 b. 40
c. 60 d. 305
e. 255 f. 8
g. 6 h. 10
i. 162 j. 18

Page 120

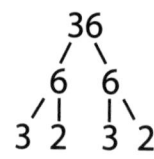

a.
```
    14
   /  \
  7    2
```
14 = 7 x 2
prime factors: 7, 2

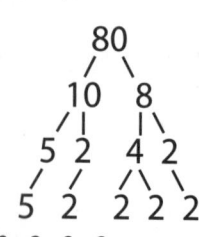

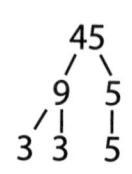

b.
```
    6
   / \
  3   2
```
6 = 3 x 2
prime factors: 3, 2

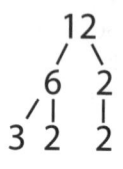

c.
```
       12
      /  \
     6    2
    /|
   3 2
```
12 = 2 x 2 x 3
prime factors: 2, 2, 3

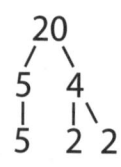

d.
```
      20
     /  \
    5    4
    |   / \
    5  2   2
```
20 = 5 x 2 x 2
prime factors: 2, 5, 5

e.
```
    21
   /  \
  3    7
```
21 = 3 x 7
prime factors: 3, 7

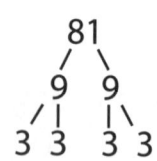

f.
```
       81
      /  \
     9    9
    /|    |\
   3 3   3 3
```
81 = 3 x 3 x 3 x 3
prime factors: 3, 3, 3, 3

g.
```
    49
   /  \
  7    7
```
49 = 7 x 7
prime factors: 7, 7

h.
```
        80
       /  \
      10   8
     /|   /|
    5 2  4 2
        /|
       2 2
```
(with 5 2 under 10 and 2 2 2 under 8)
80 = 5 x 2 x 2 x 2 x 2
prime factors: 5, 2, 2, 2, 2

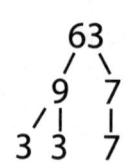

i.
```
       63
      /  \
     9    7
    /|
   3 3    7
```
63 = 7 x 3 x 3
prime factors: 7, 3, 3

j.
```
       45
      /  \
     9    5
    /|
   3 3    5
```
45 = 3 x 3 x 5
prime factors: 3, 3, 5

k.
```
       36
      /  \
     6    6
    /|   /|
   3 2  3 2
```
36 = 3 x 2 x 3 x 2
prime factors: 3, 2, 3, 2

Page 123

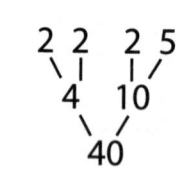

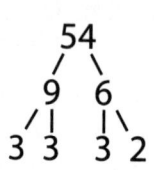

a.
```
   2 2   2 5
    \|   |/
     4  10
      \ /
      40
```
40

b.
```
       54
      /  \
     9    6
    /|   /|
   3 3  3 2
```
54 = 3 x 3 x 3 x 2
prime factors: 3, 3, 3, 2

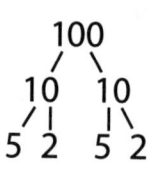

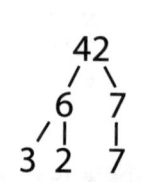

c.
```
   3 3   3 3
    \|   |/
     9    9
      \  /
       81
```
81

d.
```
       28
      /  \
     7    4
     |   /|
     7  2 2
```

e.
```
      100
     /    \
    10    10
    /|    |\
   5 2   5 2
```

f.
```
       42
      /  \
     6    7
    /|    |
   3 2    7
```

Page 124 Lesson 25 Quiz

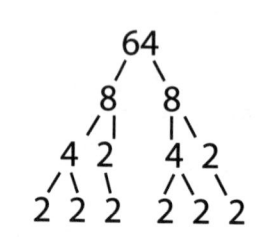

a.
```
    15
   /  \
  5    3
```
15 = 5 x 3

b.
```
       18
      /  \
     9    2
    /|
   3 3    2
```
18 = 3 x 3 x 2

c.
```
    25
   /  \
  5    5
```
25 = 5 x 5

d.
```
          64
         /  \
        8    8
       /|    |\
      4 2   4 2
     /|    /|
    2 2   2 2
```
64 = 2 x 2 x 2 x 2 x 2 x 2

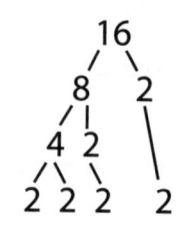

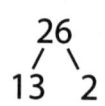

e.
```
       16
      /  \
     8    2
    /|
   4 2
  /|
 2 2         2
```
16 = 2 x 2 x 2 x 2

f.
```
    26
   /  \
  13   2
```
26 = 13 x 2

g. 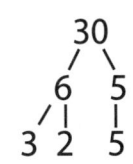
```
      30
     /  \
    6    5
   /|\   |
  3 2   5
```
30 = 5 x 2 x 3

h. 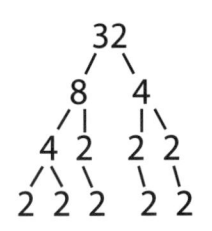
```
        32
       /  \
      8    4
    /|\   /|\
   4 2   2 2
  /|\
 2 2
```
32 = 2 x 2 x 2 x 2 x 2

i. 
```
    35
   /  \
  7    5
```
35 = 7 x 5

j. 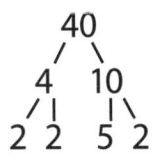
```
        40
       /  \
      4    10
     /|\   /|\
    2 2   5 2
```
40 = 2 x 2 x 2 x 5

Page 126
a. $3.11 b. $3.03 c. $0.58
d. $0.43 e. $18.14 f. $8.50
g. $1.05 h. $9.20 i. $0.92
j. $8.40 k. $0.84 l. $2.10
m. $2.50 n. $4.03 o. $1.50

Page 127
a. 7.7 b. 3.85
c. 21.0 d. 2.3 e. 51.3
f. 4.2 g. 6.0 h. 513.0
i. 5.1 j. 3.1 k. 3.0

Page 128
a. 0.87 b. 13.03
c. 10.58 d. 2.43
e. 5.3 f. 6.1
g. 210.0 h. 6.0
i. 6.5 j. 1.17
k. 3.3 l. 3.1
m. 3.8 n. 6.6
o. 5.63 p. 3.6
q. 20.1 r. 0.65
s. 4.2 t. 21.0

Page 129
a. 500.80 ÷ 40 = 12.52 hours
b. B.

c. 4.2
d. 5.3, 6
e. 9
f. $8 ÷ $1.65 = 4 tapes

Page 130 Lesson 26 Quiz
a. 6.12 b. 8.41
c. 0.25 d. 1.5
e. 1.5 f. 8.6
g. 2.3 h. 41.2
i. 1.6 j. 55.0

Page 132 Pretest
Lesson 12: 84, 147
Lesson 13: 3, 5
Lesson 14: 1,280, 1,530
Lesson 15: 2,040, 1,482
Lesson 16: 1,000, 2,400
Lesson 17: 40, 40
Lesson 18: 4, 5
Lesson 19: 6, 7
Lesson 20: 116, 2
Lesson 21: 30, 60, 90, 120; 40, 80, 120; LCM = 120
6, 12; 4, 8, 12; LCM = 12

Page 133 Pretest
Lesson 22: 2.00, 6.39
Lesson 23: $12.00, $140.00
Lesson 24: 300, 80
Lesson 25: 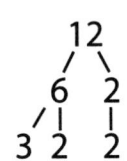
```
      12
     /  \
    6    2
   /|\
  3 2
```
12 = 2 x 2 x 3

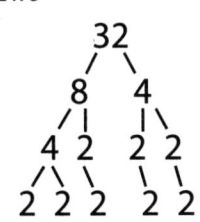

```
        32
       /  \
      8    4
    /|\   /|\
   4 2   2 2
  /|\
 2 2
```
32 = 2 x 2 x 2 x 2 x 2
Lesson 26: 9.2, 2.3

Page 134 Cumulative Test
a. 0 b. 3 c. 20 d. 28
e. 48 f. 6 g. 9 h. 8
i.
② 4 5 6
9 ⑪ 15 ⑲
21 22 ㉙ 34
45 ㊅⑦

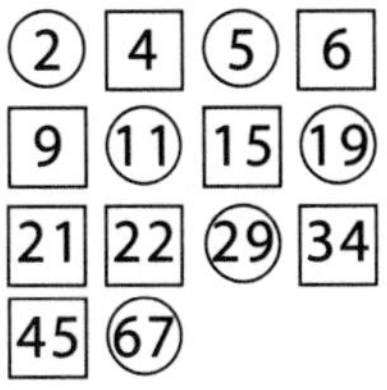

j. 480 k. 480 l. 672
m. 2,304 n. 3.25 o. 150.75
p. 13 q. 2 r. 2
s. 250
t. 63¢ u. $280 v. $107.59
w. 40 x. 500 y. 500
z. 4 aa. 7 bb. 7
cc. 3 dd. 6.45
ee. 4: 4, 8, 12
    6: 6 12
    LCM = 12
ff. 1/9 = 2/18; 1/6 = 3/18; 2/18 + 3/18 = 5/18
gg.
```
      30
     /  \
    3    10
         /|\
        5 2
  (3)
```
```
       100
      /   \
    10    10
   /|\   /|\
  5 2   5 2
```

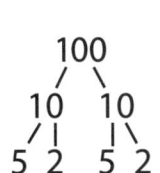

Notes